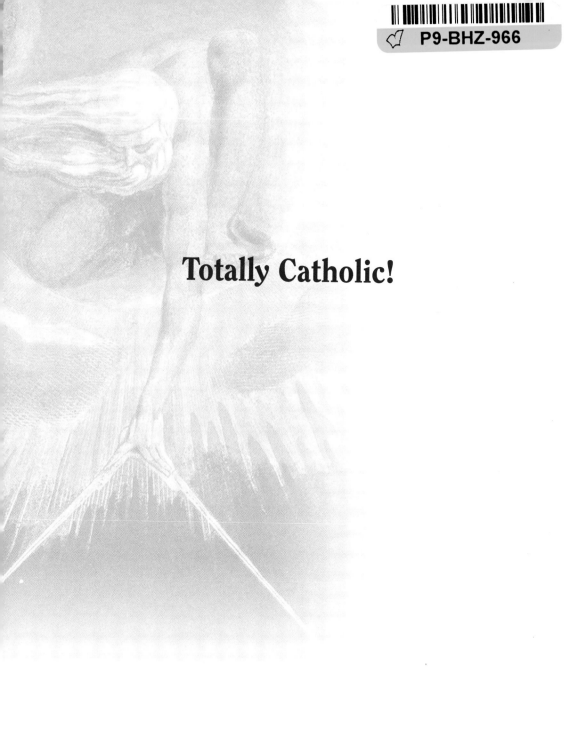

Totally Catholic!

A Catechism for Kids
and Their Parents
and Teachers

Mary Kathleen Glavich, SND

Pauline
BOOKS & MEDIA
Boston

Nihil Obstat:
Sister Mary McCormick, OSU, PhD
Censor Deputatus
Imprimatur:
✠ Most Reverend Richard G. Lennon, MTh, MA
Bishop of Cleveland
Given at Cleveland, Ohio on July 12 2012.

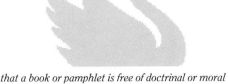

The Nihil Obstat and Imprimatur are official declarations that a book or pamphlet is free of doctrinal or moral error. No implication is contained therein that those who have granted the Nihil Obstat and Imprimatur agree with the contents, opinions, or statements expressed.

Library of Congress Cataloging-in-Publication Data

Glavich, Mary Kathleen.
  Totally Catholic! : a catechism for kids and their parents and teachers / Mary Kathleen Glavich.
    p. cm.
  Includes index.
  ISBN-13: 978-0-8198-7479-5
  ISBN-10: 0-8198-7479-5
  1. Catechetics--Catholic Church. 2. Catholic Church--Catechisms--English. 3. Christian education of children. 4. Catholic Church--Doctrines. I. Title.
  BX1968.G53 2013
  238'.2--dc23
                              2012027873

The Scripture quotations contained herein are from the *New Revised Standard Version Bible: Catholic Edition*, copyright © 1989, 1993, Division of Christian Education of the National Council of the Churches of Christ in the United States of America. Used by permission. All rights reserved.

References to the *Cathechism of the Catholic Church* have been adapted for children from the English translation of the *Catechism of the Catholic Church* for use in the United States of America, copyright © 1994, United States Catholic Conference, Inc. — Libreria Editrice Vaticana.

The English translation of The Apostles' Creed from *The Roman Missal* © 2010, International Commission on English in the Liturgy Corporation. All rights reserved.

Cover and interior design by Mary Joseph Peterson, FSP

Published by Pauline Books & Media, 50 Saint Pauls Avenue, Boston, MA 02130-3491

Printed in the U.S.A.

TC VSAUSAPEOILL2-2610039 7479-5

www.pauline.org

Pauline Books & Media is the publishing house of the Daughters of St. Paul, an international congregation of women religious serving the Church with the communications media.

3 4 5 6 7 8 9   19 18 17 16 15

Contents

1 What Is Faith? 4

2 What Is God Like? 9

3 What Has God Revealed? 15

4 How Is the Bible God's Letter to Us? 21

5 What Is the Trinity? 27

6 Why Did God Create? 32

7 Why Aren't We in Paradise? 37

8 Who Is Jesus? 43

9 How Did God Become Man? 49

10 What Was Jesus's Life Like? 55

11 How Did Jesus Teach? 61

12 How Were Jesus's Miracles Signs of the Kingdom? 66

13 Why Did Jesus Die? 71

14 What Does Jesus's Resurrection Mean? 77

15 Who Is the Holy Spirit? 83

16 What Is the Church? 89

17 What Is the Communion of Saints? 95

18 Why Is Mary Special? 100

19 What Will Happen at the End of the World? 106

20 ᔰ Why Is Liturgy Important? 112

21 ᔰ What Is Baptism? 118

22 ᔰ Why Be Confirmed? 124

23 ᔰ Why Is the Eucharist Wonderful? 130

24 ᔰ What Is the Sacrament of Penance? 136

25 ᔰ What Does the Anointing of the Sick Do? 142

26 ᔰ What Is Holy Orders? 148

27 ᔰ What Is Matrimony? 153

28 ᔰ How Can We Make Good Choices? 158

29 ᔰ Why Did God Give Us Laws? 164

30 ᔰ How Do We Love God Above All? 170

31 ᔰ Why Do We Treat God's Name With Respect? 176

32 ᔰ How Do We Keep the Lord's Day Holy? 181

33 ᔰ Who Deserves Our Respect and Obedience? 187

34 ᔰ Why Do We Respect Life? 192

35 ᔰ Why Did God Make Us Male and Female? 197

36 ᔰ What Is Involved in Honesty? 203

37 ᔰ Why Is Truth Important? 209

38 ᔰ What Is Prayer? 215

39 ᔰ What Does the Our Father Really Mean? 221

Appendixes ᔰ 227

    1. How Catholics Live 227

    2. How Catholics Pray 231

Index ᔰ 240

Pauline Books & Media is proud to present this wonderful new resource for family faith formation. In *Totally Catholic!*, Sr. Mary Kathleen Glavich, SND, has prepared a masterful text that imparts the entire faith as found in the *Catechism of the Catholic Church* in a way that reaches out to the young and not-so-young drawing them into the beauty and riches of belief. With her well-known genius, Sr. Kathleen offers the reader not only the content of our faith, but she also weaves in occasions for life response and prayer.

Knowledge is not enough for faith to be alive, we need to engage in the works of faith and we need a personal relationship with our God. When I say, "I am totally Catholic," I mean my whole self, mind, will, and heart is one with Christ. This is our hope and our prayer for you.

— Sister Mary Lea Hill, FSP
Editor

Dear Parents, Guardians, and Teachers,

Our Catholic faith infuses this life with meaning, gives us values to live by, and offers hope for an eternal life. It is a precious gift that we want to pass on to our children. In 1994, the *Catechism of the Catholic Church* was first published to summarize the essential teaching of our faith in light of today's world. It has four parts, or pillars: creed, liturgy, Christian way of life (commandments), and Christian prayer, notably the Our Father. This book is for adults.

Totally Catholic! is based on this catechism and translates its Gospel message for children. Besides simpler language, *Totally Catholic!* has stories, tidbits of information, examples, and a format that will engage young minds and hearts. Scripture is woven throughout the text, most clearly as a feature in each chapter. Also each chapter presents a saint as a role model for young Christians. Both the Scripture feature and the saint feature further develop the chapter's theme.

Although *Totally Catholic!* serves as a good reference book in the home or classroom, it is most suitable as a resource for children to study their Catholic faith more deeply. If you are using this book as a "catch-up" text to help prepare older children for the sacraments, you'll want to take advantage of these chapter components:

- creative activities suggested
- questions for discussion or reflection
- a prayer that introduces the children to the rich variety of prayer forms

The two sections in the back of the book, "How Catholics Live" and "How Catholics Pray," both contain material for reference.

Keep in mind as you teach that it's more important to talk to God about your children than to talk to your children about God. Furthermore, your example is more influential than any book. As Pope Paul VI pointed out, people today are more apt to listen to witnesses than to teachers, and if they do listen to teachers, it is because they are witnesses. This is especially true for children.

May the Holy Spirit, our Teacher and Counselor, be with you, inspiring you to be an effective apostle to the child or children in your care.

— *Mary Kathleen Glavich, SND*

Dear Child of God, ● ● ● ● ● ● ● ●

I have a new computer capable of doing many fantastic things. With this computer came a manual that explains how it works, but I haven't read it yet. Wouldn't it be silly if I never read the manual? For the most part, my computer would be wasted.

If you are a Catholic or about to become one, you have a tremendous gift—far greater than a computer. Our Catholic faith enriches our lives and gives us purpose. This book explains what it means to be a Catholic. It contains what we believe and how we live as members of the community of believers. Catholics are Christians, that is, we are followers of Jesus Christ, the Son of God. He taught us how to have a full life and, more important, by his death and rising, he won eternal life for us.

Today Jesus teaches us through his Church. This Church wrote a catechism for adults. The word *catechism* means "to echo." A catechism is a book that hands on the truths of the faith that have been echoed down the centuries from Jesus, through generations of people, to you. *Totally Catholic!* is this catechism adapted for kids your age. I hope it will make you eager to learn more about our faith.

By reading this book, you will better understand and appreciate being a Catholic. You will have the knowledge and values necessary to continue to grow as a disciple of Christ. God bless you!

— *Sister Mary Kathleen*

● ● ● ● ● ● ● ● ● ● ● ● ● ● ●

What Is Faith?

Catechism *A longing for God is written in our hearts (cf. no. 27).*

Did you know that our sun is one star in the Milky Way galaxy, which has at least 200 billion other stars? That there are more than 100 billion galaxies in what we can see of the universe? That our universe is more than 13 billion years old? Looking up at the stars at night, don't you wonder: Where did everything come from? Why am I here, living on planet earth?

We Catholics can answer questions like these because we have **faith** or belief. We believe in God, the Supreme Being who loves us and communicates with us. We believe that in Jesus, God came to earth and taught us. And we believe that God teaches us today through the Church that Jesus began. Your parents have probably passed on this faith to you. You will learn more about the Catholic faith in this book. Faith will unlock for you some of the mysteries of the universe. It will also help you live a good life so that you can enjoy an everlasting life in heaven.

God Exists

Faith in God is a gift. But we have good reasons to believe in God. Here are three:

1. The wonders of and the order in creation: giraffes, fish, dogs, trees, roses, rainbows, and mountains, in fact, everything in the whole universe. Look at your marvelous body. Your eyes let you see colors and are protected by eyelashes. Your heart beats 100,000 times a day to bring your cells oxygen. Your every movement is coordinated by your nervous system. Everything is so intricate and precise. Someone very intelligent and very powerful must have figured everything out and made it. We call that someone God.

2. The knowledge of right and wrong: we know that killing and stealing are wrong and that helping others is good. There must be someone who sets in our hearts what is right. That someone is God.

3. The desire for happiness: everyone longs to be happy. We want certain things because we think they will make us happy. But nothing keeps us happy for long. That is because God made us to be with him. God alone can make us completely happy. It's as though we have a hole in our heart that God alone can fill. Only in heaven, when we're with God, will we have lasting happiness.

Brainstorm

Think about the world. What are your favorite things about it? What are your favorite things in creation?

Share about something you wanted very much. Were you totally happy when you received it? If you are no longer satisfied, do you know why?

BTW

Faith is accepting something as true because we trust the person who tells us. For example, we have faith in our doctors.

God Loves

You might feel puny compared to the universe. But in God's eyes, you are important. God made you because he wanted to share his life with you. You are God's child. God loves you. Nothing shows God's love more than the fact that God became a man like us in Jesus who died nailed to a cross for us, and rose from the dead.

A Catholic VIP

St. Augustine (354–430)

St. Augustine was born in North Africa. He was raised by a Christian mother, St. Monica. But in his search for truth, Augustine became a follower of a false religion and strayed from the Christian values his mother had taught him. Through Monica's prayers, Augustine met good teachers like St. Ambrose and turned his life around. He was finally baptized and then became a priest and later the Bishop of Hippo. Augustine wrote so many books, letters, and sermons explaining the faith, that he was named a **doctor of the Church**, a title given to a saint outstanding in guiding the Church. His most famous book is the *Confessions*, the story of his life. St. Augustine's feast day is August 28.

Faith and Prayer

If we believe in God, then we will respond to God with love. Think how much you enjoy being with your friend or someone you love. When people love each other, they think about each other and they talk to each other. Thinking about God, and talking and listening to God is called **prayer**. In this book you will learn several ways to pray. Through prayer your love for God will grow.

The Saints

Jesus, who is God in human form, told us to have faith. He said that whoever believes in him will have eternal life. **Saints** are people who had great faith and lived like Jesus lived and taught. They were holy and full of love for God and others. The Church has declared that some of them are in heaven. The saints are examples for us. You will meet a few of them in these pages.

BTW

Of the more than 7 billion people in the world, about one third are Christian. About half of those Christians are Catholic.

Scripture Link

Appearance to Thomas

After Jesus rose from the dead, he appeared to the apostles. Thomas wasn't there. When the other apostles told him they had seen Jesus, Thomas couldn't accept it. He said he wouldn't believe until he saw and touched the wounds on Jesus's hands, feet, and side. A week later Jesus returned and this time Thomas was present. Jesus invited Thomas to touch his wounds and believe. Thomas declared, "My Lord and my God!" Then Jesus said, "Blessed are those who have not seen and yet have come to believe."

(cf. Jn 20:24–29)

The Creed

A **creed** is a summary of beliefs. At Sunday Mass we pray the Nicene Creed or the Apostles' Creed. The first part of this book explains the truths we say that we believe when we pray the Apostles' Creed. This creed is based on the teaching of the **apostles**. These were the first followers of Jesus and the leaders of the early Church. The **pope**, who is the head of the Church, and other **bishops** are their successors. They continue to teach us about the faith. Our Catholic faith is the same throughout the world.

The Catholic Life

The next part of the book introduces you to the ways Catholics worship God together. Then there are chapters that explain how Catholics live according to God's laws. The final chapters explore ways to pray. This book will help you have a living faith that you will want to share with others.

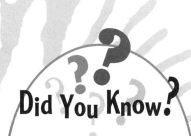

Did You Know?

Someone who dies for the faith is called a *martyr*. This word is Greek for "witness."

From My Heart

Here is an act of faith:

"My God, I believe in you and all that your Church teaches, because you have said it, and your word is true. Amen."

Now Act!

Write your own creed or write a creed with your family. And discuss together how your home can reflect that you are Catholic.

Recap

• **Faith is belief that God exists.**

• **Reasons for faith are creation, our sense of right and wrong, and our longing for happiness.**

• **We develop a relationship with God through prayer.**

What Is God Like?

Catechism *God is the one who is, who has every good quality to the full, and who has no beginning or end (cf. no. 213).*

When we think about the fact that God is pure spirit, what comes to mind? Sometimes it's tough to understand how God is always with us watching over us, because we can't see or hear or touch God. God is a pure **spirit**, which means that he has no physical body and is invisible. God is an uncreated spirit. In other words, no one made God. He had no beginning. Also, God will always exist. God is **eternal**, that is, he always was and always will be.

One God

If you studied or have read about Greek and Roman mythology, you know that it was common for people to believe in many gods and goddesses. These divine persons were thought to be like us with the same virtues and faults that we have. Other early people believed that objects like trees or things they carved were gods. These false gods are called **idols**. Through the Jewish people, we came to believe that there is only one God, the Supreme Being, who is to be adored and loved.

Holy God

Take the word *God*, stretch it out, and it becomes "good." That is fitting because God is good. There is nothing evil about him. We say that God is **holy**. Think of any good quality, or perfection, such as kindness, and God has it without limit, that is, to an **infinite** degree. For example, God is infinitely kind. God, however, is basically a mystery. He is beyond anything we can imagine. The words we use to describe him are only a shadow of what our great God is really like. We do, though, get glimpses of God's qualities. Anything you make is a reflection of you. It tells something about you. Similarly, what God has made teaches us about him. Everything in the universe speaks about God.

BTW

Omni means "all." God is **omnipresent** (everywhere), **omnipotent** (all-powerful), and **omniscient** (all-knowing).

God's Presence

God is present everywhere, keeping everything in existence. You could go to the ends of the earth or the farthest star, and God would still be there. He is with you this moment. Better still, God is present within you! He is the source of life.

God's Power

Have you ever been to the ocean and seen waves crashing on the shore and against rocks? The ocean is mighty and wide. It speaks to us of God's power. God rules everything and can do anything. Nothing is impossible for God. He is all-powerful.

Scripture Link

God's Personal Name

The Israelites were slaves in Egypt. One day when Moses led his father-in-law's sheep to Mount Horeb, he saw a bush on fire that did not burn up. When Moses approached it, God called out to him and told him to remove his sandals because the place was holy ground. Then God told Moses to ask Pharaoh, king of Egypt, to let his people go free. Moses asked God his name. God replied, "I am who I am." This is God's personal, mysterious name. It means "He who is," the source of all being. It also means "I am with you," which shows God's faithful love for us.

(cf. Ex 3:1–15)

Did You Know?

The study of God is called **theology**. *Theo* means "God."

God's Knowledge

Every day scientists discover new things about the world. For example, in 2009, they found that birds are able to fly because their bone structure keeps their lungs from collapsing. Whoever designed birds and the countless other marvels in the universe had to be very intelligent. Of course, it was God, who knows all things. Nothing is hidden from God.

A God of Truth

How do you feel when someone lies to you? We always seek to know the truth. The sciences help us discover what is real. God always speaks the truth, and God keeps his promises. We can trust God not to deceive us. What our faith tells us doesn't contradict what we learn from science. There is only one truth.

A God of Beauty

When we see a beautiful flower or hear a beautiful piece of music, our hearts are glad. The beauty of the earth is only an inkling of God's beauty, which we will behold in heaven.

A God of Justice

Justice means giving everyone what is due to him or her. God is fair. He punishes evil and rewards good. We will see this at a final judgment at the end of the world.

BTW

Atheism (AY-thee-is-uhm) is belief in no God. **Agnosticism** (ag-NOS-ti-siz-uhm) is to be unsure of God's existence.

Did You Know?

Out of respect for God's holiness, Jewish people never say or write God's name. They use the word *Lord*, and they write G-d.

Brainstorm

How many things in nature can you think of that show the power of God? How many things reflect his kindness?

A God of Mercy

Although God is just, he also forgives. By the redemption, he forgave the human race; in the Scriptures we see how often he forgave his people, the Israelites; and he willingly forgives us whenever we ask. God has compassion for us when we are sorry for doing wrong. With love, he offers us another chance.

A God of Love

God loves us more than a mother loves her child. His love is everlasting. No matter what we do, God faithfully loves us. St. John said, "God *is* love."

An Unchanging God

God never changes. For all eternity he has the perfections you have just read about. This wonderful Being is who we came from and the One to whom we are going.

A Catholic VIP

St. Thomas Aquinas (1225–1274)

St. Thomas was born into a wealthy family. When he joined the religious community of the Dominicans, his family was upset and imprisoned him for a year in their castle. But Thomas rejoined the Dominicans and went on to become a brilliant Christian thinker and writer. He is known for the *Summa Theologiae*, five volumes that summarize theology. Near the end of his life, St. Thomas concluded that all he had written was as worthless as straw compared to true knowledge of God. St. Thomas is a doctor of the Church. His feast day is January 28.

From My Heart

Focus on God, who is all around you and in your heart. For a few minutes just be quiet and enjoy being in God's presence. Then pray, "O God, I adore you, I believe in you, I hope in you, and I love you."

Now Act!

In Scripture the Israelites had names for God, such as Shield, the Holy One, Shepherd, King, Master, and Rock. Choose one of these, or make up your own name for God, and write a prayer to him, calling him by that name. When you speak to God, address him by this special name.

Recap

● ● ● ● ● ● ● ● ● ● ● ● ● ● ● ● ● ● ● ●

- **There is one God, a pure, uncreated spirit who is eternal and unchanging.**

- **God is everywhere, is all-powerful, and knows all things.**

- **God has all perfections to an infinite degree. He is just, truthful, merciful, and loving.**

3

What Has God Revealed?

Catechism *Little by little, by actions and words, God has revealed the mystery of who he is (cf. no. 69).*

Children have always played hide-and-seek. A holy man named Meister Eckhart once said that God is like someone hiding who clears his throat in order to give himself away. You've seen how we can know about God from creation. God has made it even easier to know him. Gradually he has revealed himself and his plan for us. This is called **revelation** (rev-uh-LAY-shuhn). God has spoken to us and entered into solemn agreements with us known as **covenants** (KUHV-uh-nuhnts). Constantly God calls us to a loving relationship with him.

Early Revelation

God's goal was to live with human beings forever. He showed himself to our first parents, Adam and Eve, and shared his divine life with them. After they sinned God did not abandon them. In his infinite goodness and mercy, he chose to revise his plan. He promised to save the human race and make life with him possible again. Later, in the time of Noah, God was so offended by the sins of the people that he planned to begin his world all over again. But God saved Noah and his family

15

from the great flood. God made a covenant with Noah and all living things to show mercy, and not destroy the world by floods again (cf. Gen 1–9).

The Chosen People

In about 2000 B.C., God spoke to a man named Abram. God changed his name to Abraham, which means "the father of many nations." God entered into a covenant with Abraham, promising to bless all nations through him. Abraham and his descendants were God's chosen people, the Israelites, later called Jews (cf. Gen 12–25:11).

When the Israelites were slaves in Egypt for centuries, God came to their rescue. He sent Moses to tell the Pharaoh to free them. Ten plagues helped persuade the king to let the Israelites go. Then Moses led the Israelites through the desert to the land God promised them. On the way, God made a covenant with the Israelites. God gave them his law, the Ten Commandments, and they agreed to do whatever he said. The Israelites' great escape is called the **Exodus** (EK-suh-duhs).

BTW

Abraham and his immediate descendants are called **patriarchs** (PAY-tree-arkz), which means "chief fathers." They include his son Isaac, his grandson Jacob, and Jacob's twelve sons.

Did You Know?

Jewish history shines with great women like Sarah, Deborah, Ruth, Judith, Esther, and Mary, the mother of Jesus.

Brainstorm

What Bible stories do you know? What do they tell us about God?

Once the Israelites were in their land, God spoke to them through prophets. God formed his people, calling them over and over to be faithful to him and his law. He foretold a new covenant and salvation for the world. The Jews kept hope alive (cf. Ex 1–20:21).

God's Greatest Revelation

God's final and greatest revelation was Jesus. In the **Incarnation** (in-kahr-NAY-shuhn), when the Son of God came to earth as man, God revealed himself fully to us. Jesus is the ultimate Word of God. By his own life and teachings, he showed us how God wants us to live. There will be no new revelation. Together as a Church we grow in our understanding of what God has revealed.

One Revelation, Two Channels

How do we know what God revealed? God's greatest revelation comes in Jesus. Christians understand this revelation through two channels: Scripture and tradition. Jesus commanded his apostles, his closest followers, to teach his Gospel. Their teaching handed on God's revelation to others. It has come down to us through the successors of the apostles, the bishops, who continue to teach. This teaching is called **tradition** and is found in the life and worship of the Church that Jesus founded. Second, revelation has been written down in **Scripture**, the Bible. Together tradition and Scripture form one **deposit of faith**. This deposit is like a window through which we can see God.

How do we know that what we believe about God is true? God the Holy Spirit guided the formation of both tradition and Scripture. The Holy Spirit also guides the teaching of the faith today (cf. Jn 15:26).

> ## BTW
>
> The twelve apostles are Peter, James, John, Andrew, Philip, Bartholomew, Matthew, Thomas, James, Jude Thaddeus, Simon, and Matthias (who replaced Judas).

A Catholic VIP

St. Peter (?–64)

Simon, a fisherman, was called to be an apostle along with his brother Andrew. Jesus changed Simon's name to Cephas, or "Rock." The name Peter comes from the Greek word for rock. Once when Jesus asked, "Who do you say I am?" Peter responded, "You are Christ the Son of the living God." Jesus then said he would build his Church on this rock and give Peter the keys of the kingdom. This meant Peter would lead the Church. Peter preached and cured people, and was imprisoned for it. He was sentenced to death on a cross. Feeling unworthy to die as Jesus did, Peter asked to be crucified upside down. The great Basilica of St. Peter in Rome was built over his burial site. St. Peter's feast day is June 29.

The Church as Teacher

Jesus gave Church leaders authority to teach and interpret the Word of God. This authority is called **magisterium** (maj-uh-STEER-ee-uhm). Sometimes the Church states a matter about faith in a definite way. This official statement is known as a **dogma**. It is something every Catholic believes. Catholic teachings in general are called **doctrines**.

Our pope is the successor of Peter, the apostle Jesus appointed to lead his Church. The pope is the bishop of Rome and the visible head of the Church. He and the other bishops teach through sermons, letters, and meetings. A meeting of all the bishops in the world is called an **ecumenical** (ek-yoo-MEN-i-kuhl) **council**.

BTW

Other names for the pope are Holy Father, Vicar (Agent) of Christ, and Supreme Pontiff. (*Pons* is Latin for "bridge." The pope is like a bridge, or connection, between God in heaven and people on earth.)

Scripture Link

The Sacrifice of Isaac

Although Abraham and his wife Sarah were old, God promised him many descendants. Finally they had a son, Isaac. But one day God tested Abraham's faith. Back then people offered sacrifices as gifts to honor their gods. They offered the produce of the land or animal sacrifices. God told Abraham to take Isaac to a mountain and sacrifice him. Abraham didn't understand why God asked this, but he had faith and obeyed. After Abraham had built an altar and set Isaac on it, he drew out his knife. Suddenly an angel stopped him, and Abraham found a ram to offer instead. Through this, God taught the importance of obedience and that he didn't want human sacrifice.

(cf. Gen 22:1–14)

Did You Know?

The last Church council was the Second Vatican Council (1962–1965). Sixteen documents about our Catholic faith came from it.

From My Heart

Ask God to open your eyes to see his truths, to open your ears to hear his Word, and to open your heart to respond with love.

Now Act!

Find a smooth rock. With
a permanent marker or paint
write, "God loves me" on it.
Put it where it will remind you
how precious you are to God.

You might want
to make another one
to give away to a friend.

Recap

- God revealed himself and his plan and made covenants with us.

- After humans sinned, God promised to save the human race.

- God told Abraham that all nations would be blessed through
  his offspring.

- God brought the Israelites out of slavery in Egypt to the Promised
  Land. He made a covenant with them and gave them his law.

- God's greatest revelation was Jesus Christ.

- We know revelation through the Church's deposit of faith:
  Scripture and tradition.

4

How Is the Bible God's Letter to Us?

Catechism *In the Holy Bible our heavenly Father lovingly meets us and speaks with us (cf. no. 104).*

Can you answer these?

♣ What is the best-selling book of all time?

♣ What book has been translated into 2,454 languages?

♣ What book did George Washington kiss at his inauguration?

♣ What book is the origin of the expressions "a good Samaritan," "a leopard can't change its spots," "the blind leading the blind," and "the patience of Job"?

You've probably guessed that the answer to all the questions is the Bible. You hear readings from the Bible at every Mass. You might have your own Bible. There are good reasons why this book is famous and loved. Imagine going to your computer and finding an e-mail from God to you. Wouldn't you be surprised? What do you think God would write? Actually God does communicate with you through writing. God is the author of the Bible, a book in which God speaks personally to you. Another name for the Bible is **Sacred Scripture**, which means holy writing. People physically wrote the words, but God influenced them to say what he wanted. This divine influence is called **inspiration**. Although the Bible is a collection of seventy-three different books, God sends one strong message in it: "I love you." In the Bible, over and over again God tells us of his love for us and shows us his love by great saving acts.

A Two-Part Story

The Bible tells the story of God's relationship with the human race in two parts. This first part, which has forty-six books, is the **Old Testament**. It begins with creation stories and traces the history of God's chosen people, the Israelites. It was through them that God first made a covenant with us and through them he promised a Savior. The second part of the Bible, which has twenty-seven books, is the **New Testament**. This part tells how God sent the Savior, Jesus. The Gospels recount the life and teachings of Jesus, and the Acts of the Apostles gives the history of the early Church. It also includes letters of the first Christians that explain the faith. The last book, Revelation, contains visions that foretell the triumph of Christ.

Both of the Bible's two parts reveal what God is like, who Jesus is, how God saved us, and how to live wisely.

How to Read the Bible

Like a library, the Bible has different kinds of books, or literary forms, such as historical writing, stories, poetry, and letters. The Church tells us to be mindful of the kind of writing it is as we read each book of the Bible. For example, Jesus told para-

BTW

In a Bible reference the name of the book is given followed by the chapter number and then the verse number. John 15:14 means the Gospel of John, chapter 15, verse 14. Can you find this verse in your Bible?

Did You Know?

We are to honor the Bible as we honor the Eucharist, which is the Body and Blood of Christ.

bles, which are fictional stories that illustrate a teaching. You shouldn't think, then, that they actually happened. The Church also tells us to read the books with awareness of the culture of the people who wrote them. Christ, who is the Word of God, helps us understand Scripture through the Holy Spirit. The Church interprets Scripture for us.

Now Act!

The Bible is the way God chose to communicate his teachings, expectations, and love to us. Prepare a place in your home where you will keep the Bible. Make this a place of honor, but remember that the Bible is to be read, so make the Bible easily accessible. Having God's Word in your home will bring many blessings to the family.

Did You Know?

The symbol for Mark is a lion, Matthew's is a man, Luke's is an ox, and John's is an eagle.

The Gospels

The heart of Scripture is the four **Gospels**. *Gospel* means "Good News." The Gospels are about Jesus, his life and work and his death and resurrection. Each Gospel is a portrait of Jesus. It tells his story from a particular point of view and for a certain audience. The first three—the Gospels of Matthew, Mark, and Luke—are similar. We call them the **Synoptics** (sin-OP-tics), which means "same view." The Gospel of John is unique. The authors credited with writing the Gospels are called **evangelists** (i-VAN-juh-lists), from the Greek for "Good News."

**St. Luke
(First century)**

The evangelist St. Luke was St. Paul's companion and a physician. The Gospel of Luke has some of the most loved stories, including those about the birth of Jesus. Luke shows the compassionate Jesus who loves all people, especially the poor. His Gospel is called the Gospel of the Spirit, the Gospel of Prayer, the Gospel of Women, the Gospel of the Poor, and the Gospel of Joy. Besides his Gospel, Luke wrote the Acts of the Apostles, considered to be part two of his Gospel. St. Luke's feast day is October 18.

The Letters

There are twenty-one letters, or **epistles** (i-PIS-uhls), in the Bible. Most of these were written by St. Paul. He began many churches in the first century. Because Paul preached the Gospel to the gentiles (non-Jews), he is known as the Apostle to the Gentiles. Here are the first fourteen letters, which are named for the people to whom they were sent: Romans, 1 Corinthians, 2 Corinthians, Galatians, Ephesians, Philippians, Colossians, 1 Thessalonians, 2 Thessalonians, 1 Timothy, 2 Timothy, Titus, Philemon, Hebrews.

The other letters were written by St. James, St. Peter, St. John, and St. Jude.

BTW

Here is a jingle to help you remember the first fourteen letters in order so that you can locate verses in them easily:
Ro-Co-Co
Gal-Eph-Phi
Col-Thess-Thess
Tim-Tim-Ti
Phil-Heb

Praying with the Bible

Try reading a few verses from the Bible every day. Then think about them. Listen to what God is saying to you personally through the gift of his word.

Scripture Link

A House Built on Rock

Jesus told a parable, or story, about living by his Word. A person who acts on God's Word is like a wise man who built his house on rock. When rains fell, floods came, and wind battered the house, it did not fall. Someone who does not act on God's Word is like a foolish man who built his house on sand. When a storm comes, this house collapses.

(cf. Mt 7:24–27)

BTW

Catholic Bibles have more books than Protestant Bibles. The Church decided on the **canon**, or list of divinely inspired books, in 382 A.D. and officially confirmed it in 1546.

From My Heart

The Bible's book of Psalms has 150 **psalms** (sahmz). These are prayer songs of praise, sorrow, gratitude, and petition that all Jews prayed, including Jesus and Mary. Today we pray them. Psalm 119, the longest psalm, exclaims how wonderful God's word is. Every eight verses begin with a consecutive letter of the Hebrew alphabet. Pray Psalm 119:97–105.

Now Act!

This Sunday listen carefully to the readings at Mass. The first reading is from a book of the Old Testament. The second reading is from one of the New Testament letters. Then there is a psalm and a reading from one of the Gospels. Try to remember these readings, which together are called the Liturgy of the Word. Did you notice a theme that connected the readings?

Recap

• •

- **God is the author of the Bible, Sacred Scripture.**

- **The first part of the Bible, the Old Testament, tells the history of God's chosen people.**

- **The second part of the Bible, the New Testament, recounts the life of Jesus in four Gospels and the history of the early Church.**

- **We read the Bible aware of its literary forms and Jewish culture.**

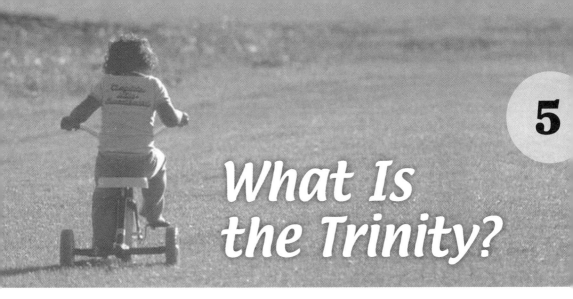

What Is the Trinity?

5

Catechism *There is one God, who is, however, a Most Holy Trinity: the Father, his only Son, and the Holy Spirit (cf. no. 233).*

Life is full of mysteries. The greatest mystery of all is the **Most Holy Trinity**. *Tri* means three, as in *tricycle*. We believe that our one God is three Persons, the Father, the Son, and the Holy Spirit. The Father is God, the Son is God, and the Holy Spirit it God. Yet there is only one God. How can 1 + 1 + 1 ever equal 1? We will never understand how this can be, but we believe it on the word of Jesus.

A Central Mystery

The mystery of the Most Holy Trinity is the heart of all that Catholics believe. You were or will be baptized in the name of the Father and of the Son and of the Holy Spirit (cf. Mt 28:19). The Trinity is one mystery that we could not discover on our own. God revealed it to us. Jesus taught us about the Father and the Holy Spirit. Then the Holy Spirit came upon the Church on Pentecost and guided us to know more about God the Father and God the Son.

What We Know

The Persons in the Trinity are all God. So each Person is eternal, and each one has equal powers. The Father, though, is the source of the Son. And the Holy Spirit comes from the Father and Son together. We say that the Father *generates* the Son, who is *begotten*. The Holy Spirit *proceeds* from them both. Each Person is distinct. Although the three divine Persons are different from one another, they are one and the same God. We worship all three Persons.

Comparisons

People have tried to explain the mystery of the Trinity. For example, they compare the Trinity to an egg. There is a shell, egg white, and a yolk but one egg. St. Patrick is famous for using a shamrock to teach about the Trinity. He pointed out that although there are three leaves, there is only one shamrock. The Trinity has been compared to water, too, which has three states: liquid, solid (ice), and gas (steam). These comparisons help, but remember we can never understand this deep mystery of the Godhead.

St. Augustine once saw a boy on a beach pouring water into a pail. He asked, "What are you doing?" The boy replied, "I'm putting the ocean in my pail." "That's impossible," Augustine said. "No more impossible than trying to put the mystery of the Trinity in your human brain," the boy said.

Did You Know?

We celebrate Trinity Sunday on the Sunday after the feast of Pentecost Sunday.

A Catholic VIP

St. Patrick (389? – 461?)

St. Patrick is the popular patron saint of Ireland. Born in Britain, Patrick was captured by pirates and taken to Ireland. He finally escaped back to Britain and became a priest. When missionaries, people who spread the faith, were needed to go to Ireland, Patrick volunteered. He was made a bishop and sent to places where people worshiped false gods. These people were called Druids. The Druid priests resisted, but Patrick successfully brought the light of faith to Ireland. St. Patrick's feast day is March 17.

Work of the Trinity

Whatever God does, all three Persons do. They work together. However, each Person is revealed to us as having a special mission, or task. The Father is responsible for creation. The Son was sent to become a man and save the world. And the Holy Spirit is in charge of guiding the Church and making its members holy.

Life of the Blessed Trinity

The Persons in the Trinity are a family bound together in a relationship of love. Out of love, God created us to share this divine life. We call God's life in us **sanctifying grace**. Already we are joined to God on earth. God dwells within us. Our destiny is to enter fully into the life of the Trinity. This is what heaven is: union with the great and loving God who made us.

Jesus's Teachings About God

- "If you knew me, you would know my Father also" (Jn 8:19).

- "The one who sent me is true, and I declare to the world what I have heard from him" (Jn 8:26).

- "The Father is in me and I am in the Father" (Jn 10:38).

- "Those who love me will keep my word, and my Father will love them, and we will come to them and make our home with them" (Jn 14:23).

- "The Advocate [Helper], the Holy Spirit, whom the Father will send in my name, will teach you everything, and remind you of all that I have said to you" (Jn 14:26).

Did You Know?

God, who is a spirit, is not male or female. It's just a custom to speak about God in male terms because that is how God revealed himself.

Scripture Link

The Baptism of Jesus

John was a prophet who urged people to give up their sins. He had them baptized, or "washed" in the Jordan River as a sign that they had a change of heart. Before Jesus began preaching, he went to John the Baptist and asked to be baptized. When Jesus was coming out of the water, the heavens opened and the Spirit came down like a dove on him. A voice from heaven said, "You are my Son, the Beloved; with you I am well pleased."

(cf. Mk 1:9–11)

From My Heart

Pray: Glory to the Father, and to the Son, and to the Holy Spirit. As it was in the beginning is now and will be forever. Amen.

Now Act!

Draw three circles with each one overlapping the other two. Label one Father, another Son, and another Holy Spirit. In each circle write or draw something about that Person of the Blessed Trinity.

Recap

• •

- **God is a Holy Trinity, three Persons in one God: the Father, the Son, and the Holy Spirit.**

- **The three Persons are eternal and have equal powers.**

- **Although the Trinity works together, the Father is the creator, the Son is the Savior, and the Holy Spirit is the Sanctifier, who makes the Church holy.**

- **Sanctifying grace is the life of the Trinity, which is shared with us.**

6

Why Did God Create?

Catechism *God created all things because of his goodness and love (cf. no. 293).*

One day a scientist said to God, "We don't need you anymore. Science can now clone people and do all sorts of marvelous things."

"Well, let's have a contest to make a man just like I did it in the old days," God replied.

"No problem," said the scientist as he scooped up a handful of dirt.

"No, no!" said God. "Get your own dirt."

The point of this story is that God made everything out of nothing.

To **create** from nothing means to make something with no materials. Before the universe, only God existed. Then, in order to show forth his glory and share his goodness and love, God called creation into being. In Genesis, the first book of the Bible, God simply says, "Let there be," and everything in heaven and earth exists. Creation is accomplished by Father, Son, and Holy Spirit.

Two Creation Accounts

Genesis has two stories of creation. The first one is a poem in which God creates everything in six days and then rests on the seventh day.

Day one: Light

Day two: Sky

Day three: Earth and seas, plants

Day four: Sun, moon, and stars

Day five: Sea creatures and birds

Day six: Land animals, man and woman

Did You Know?

Sunday is our day of rest. On Sunday we spend more time with God and enjoy his creation.

You might ask, "How could there be light before the sun was created?" Remember, we read the Bible aware of the literary forms. This creation story is written as a poem and is not meant to be understood as a historical document.

In the second story, God made the heavens and earth. Then he formed a man, Adam, from the dust of the earth and breathed life into him. God planted a garden in Eden, or **paradise**, and put Adam in charge of it. Wanting to give Adam a partner, God made animals and birds from the dirt and had Adam name them. None was a suitable partner. So God put Adam to sleep, took one of his ribs, and formed it into a woman, Eve. She was the perfect companion for Adam. The creation story shows us that all men and women have the same dignity and are equal (cf. Gen 1:1–2:24).

Brainstorm

What needs to be done in your neighborhood to make it a more beautiful part of creation? What would make it a place of peace, justice, and love reflecting God's kingdom?

Angels

God also created **angels**, who are powerful, intelligent, spiritual beings. They are in God's presence, adoring him and acting as his servants and messengers. Each person has a guardian angel as a protector and guide through life on earth. You can pray to your guardian angel for help. Angels who rebelled against God are called **devils**, or evil spirits. They are now in hell separated from God. They try to get us to join them by sinning.

Did You Know?

We help bring about the kingdom of God by our good actions, our prayers, and our sufferings.

BTW

Adam is the Hebrew word for "man." *Adamah* is Hebrew for "red earth."

Human Beings

Every person—the weak, the strong, the good, and the wicked—has dignity because God made us in his own image and likeness. That means that we are spirit as well as body. Our spirit, or **soul**, enables us to think, choose, and love like God. Unlike all other creatures, we are a union of body and soul with a mind and a free will. We were created to know, love, and serve God. Our souls were made directly by God and will never die.

Scripture Link

Lesson on Trust

Jesus said, "Look at the birds. They don't work, but the heavenly Father feeds them. Aren't you of more value than they? Look at the lilies of the field. They don't work, but not even King Solomon was clothed like they are. If God clothes them, how much more will he clothe you? Don't worry. God knows what you need. Strive first for the kingdom of God, and all these things will be given you."

(cf. Mt 6:26–33)

A Good World

Because the world came from our good God, it too is good. Genesis says, "God saw everything that he had made, and indeed, it was very good" (Gen 1:31). No created thing, though, is greater than God who created it. God keeps everything in existence. Creation is God's gift to us to enjoy and to care for. But creation is not finished yet. It is being perfected until the end of time when God promised to make a new heaven and a new earth, a perfect world (cf. Rev 21:1–5).

God's Providence

God is not like a landlord who never checks on or helps his renters. No, God guides and watches over everyone, everything, and all the events in history. This care is called **Divine Providence**. Jesus taught that our heavenly Father knows all our needs, cares for us, and even counts the hairs on our head (cf. Mt 10:30)! God wants us to cooperate in carrying out his plan for the world. He leaves us free, however, to help complete his work of creation or not. The plan's goal is the **kingdom of God**, that is, when everyone lives in peace and justice and love.

A Catholic VIP

St. Francis of Assisi (1181?–1226)

Francis was the son of a wealthy cloth merchant in Italy. After being captured in a war, he took to heart Jesus's words: "Sell all you have, give to the poor, and follow me" (cf. Mt 19:21). One day Francis heard a voice say, "Repair my house." At first he thought this meant the church building, but then he realized it meant the people of God. Francis went about begging and preaching. People joined him, and he formed religious communities, who came to be known as Franciscans. Francis loved all creatures. He called them his brothers and sisters. In his poem "Canticle of the Sun," Francis tells created things to praise God. He was the first to make a Christmas manger scene with live animals. His feast day is October 4. Some parishes hold blessings of animals on this day.

From My Heart

The Word of God calls on all things in nature to bless the Lord. The Canticle of Daniel says, "Bless the Lord, you winds; sing praise to him forever." Look up this song of praise in your Bible and then write one of your own about things you are grateful for.

Visit the zoo or watch a nature program, marvel at God's work, and in your heart thank God for the wonders of our world.

Now Act!

Recap

• • • • • • • • • • • • • • • • • • • •

- **God created everything out of nothing to show his glory and share his goodness and love.**

- **The Bible has two creation stories in which God makes man and woman.**

- **God created pure spirits, the angels; some of them rebelled and are known as devils.**

- **Human beings are body and spirit. Our spirit, called a soul, enables us to think, choose, and love like God.**

- **The world is good, given to us to enjoy and care for.**

- **God cares for the world and plans a kingdom of peace, justice, and love.**

7

Why Aren't We in Paradise?

Catechism *Human beings are marked by the original sin that our first parents freely committed (cf. no. 390).*

God made us to share his wonderful life. Look at the word *live*. What do the letters spell backwards? Our first parents reversed God's plan. They sinned, which means they refused to love God and do his will. As a result, sin, suffering, and death entered God's beautiful, good world. The sin of Adam and Eve is called the **original sin**, meaning the first sin.

God's Original Plan

The first couple lived in friendship with God in a garden paradise. They enjoyed the divine life of **grace** and were holy. Therefore they lived in harmony with each other and with the rest of creation. They were free from cravings for pleasure, wealth, or power. This happy state is called **original justice**. God, however, did not force Adam and Eve to love and obey him. He gave them a **free will**. Our first parents chose to disobey God's command. We don't know what they did, but their sin shattered their relationship with God. Genesis describes the Fall of Adam and Eve in story form.

Original Sin in Genesis

In the Garden of Eden, God told Adam and Eve they could eat from any tree except the tree of the knowledge of good and evil. They were not to eat it, or they would die. One day a serpent told Eve that anyone who ate the fruit of the forbidden tree would be like God. This serpent was the devil, the liar who tempts us to sin. The fruit looked good, so Eve disobeyed God and ate it. She gave some to Adam, and he ate it too. When the couple heard their friend God moving in the garden, they hid. God knew they had acted against his will.

God spelled out the consequences of original sin. The serpent would have to crawl on his belly. The woman would bear children in pain. And the man would have to work hard on the land. All human beings would die and return to dust. But God also gave a hint of a Savior. He said that between the devil and a woman there would be conflict and her offspring would crush the devil's head. Then God sent Adam and Eve out of Eden.

Brainstorm

If you could speak to Adam and Eve, what would you say? What would you ask them? Would you have any advice for them? How would you explain how sin affected history and how it is affecting the world today? Can you explain redemption to them?

Did You Know?

The original sin we're born with is not our personal sin. Our sinful acts are called **actual sins**.

Consequences for Us

Adam and Eve had lost their original holiness. They found it hard to resist sin. There was tension between them as a couple and disharmony with creation. Because Adam is our father, all human beings are born into this sad state of original sin. It spread down to us like a computer virus. We are born without grace and with a tendency to sin, and we experience ignorance, suffering, and death. We are wounded and weakened beings. But because of our Savior, Jesus, we can hope again. He repaired the damage done by Adam. In fact, Jesus brought us more graces. We see the depths of God's love and mercy, we hear his teaching and see his example, and we can celebrate the Eucharist, where we receive Jesus into our hearts.

The Spread of Sin

The Bible shows that evil was let loose in the world. Adam and Eve had two sons, Cain and Abel. Cain was jealous of Abel and killed him. At one point later on, the only good people on earth were Noah and his family. God saved them from a great flood. Even when God made the Israelites his special people, they were unfaithful to him over and over and broke the commandments he gave them. But God remained faithful to his people.

After Jesus came, people continued to disobey God. Even St. Paul struggled against sin. He wrote, "I do not do what I want, but I do the very thing I hate" (Rom 7:15). Sound familiar? You too may find it hard to be good. We must battle against temptations all the time. Have courage, our good God gives us grace, which is supernatural (more than natural) power, to resist evil and do what's right. Grace makes us stronger than we can be on our own. It is sharing in the life of God. We receive God's grace through prayer and the sacraments.

A Catholic VIP

St. John the Baptist (First century)

John was a relative of Jesus and the prophet who prepared the way for him. John lived in the desert, clothed in animal skins and eating locusts. He called people to change their lives and follow God's law of love. As a sign that they were sorry for their sins, people would be baptized by John. When King Herod married his own brother's wife, John spoke out against this sin. So Herod imprisoned John. On Herod's birthday his wife's daughter danced so well that he offered her anything up to half his kingdom. Prompted by her mother, the girl asked for John's head on a platter. Herod had John killed. We celebrate St. John's birth on June 24 and his martyrdom on August 29.

Our Hope

Mary's Son, Jesus, by his death and resurrection, conquered evil forever. Jesus and his mother are the only people who never sinned. Because of her special role, God gave Mary the privilege of being born without original sin. We call this Mary's **immaculate conception** (i-MAK-yuh-lit kuhn-SEP-shuhn). Under this title she is the patroness of the United States.

BTW

Some pictures and statues show Mary crushing a serpent under her foot. They show Mary's role in our redemption.

Did You Know?

Another "sin story" in Genesis (chapter 11) is about people who are too proud and ambitious. They try to build a tower to heaven so everyone will admire them. To prevent such a sin, God makes them speak different languages. Their city is called Babel.

Why Evil?

You might wonder why God let Adam and Eve sin. The gift of free will that God gave them made it possible for them to love as he loves. They were free to love or not (which is sin). Without free will, we would be nothing but robots. Surprisingly, the first sin led to an even greater blessing for us: the loving mercy of God who sent his Son as Redeemer. And we now have the Church and Mary as our Mother.

Scripture Link

The Prodigal Son

Jesus told a story about a son who asks his father for his inheritance. The young man goes to a distant land and wastes the money in sinful ways. Although he finds a job caring for pigs, he is starving. He decides to return home, admit his sin, and ask his father to hire him. While he was still far off, the father spots him. He runs to meet him and hugs and kisses him. The son begins, "I have sinned. I'm unworthy to be called son." Before he can say more, the father tells his servants to bring the best robe, a ring, and sandals for his son. He directs them to kill a calf for a celebration. He exclaims, "My son was dead and is alive again!" God the Father welcomes sinners back with the same mercy and joy.

(cf. Lk 15:11–24)

BTW

The gift of God's grace makes us holy.

From My Heart

Pray the Our Father on page 231. In this prayer, which Jesus taught us, we ask that God's will be done and that he forgive us for our sins. We also ask God to keep us from temptation.

Now Act!

Find evidence of sin in the news. Pray for people suffering because of others' evil actions. Pray for the sinners too.

Read these stories in Genesis: Cain (4:1–16), the Flood (6:1–9:17), Babel (11:1–9). How does God show mercy in each case? Read the short book of Jonah in the Bible and in a sentence tell what Jonah learns about God.

Recap

● ●

- **God shared his life and grace with the first couple and they were happy.**

- **The first parents disobeyed God, committing the first sin, and were barred from heaven.**

- **Each person inherits the state of original sin with a tendency to sin.**

- **God promised a Savior through a woman, who was Mary.**

8

Who Is Jesus?

Catechism *Jesus, a Jew from Nazareth, is the eternal Son of God who became man to redeem us (cf. nos. 422–423).*

St. Ignatius encouraged using the imagination for prayer. In order to understand the love and mercy that caused God to become a human being to save us, Ignatius once proposed imagining the three Persons of the Trinity seated on a throne in heaven and looking at the earth. Father, Son, and Holy Spirit see human beings dying; they see violence and wars. With loving mercy, they decide to do something to save the human race. The Son, the Second Person of the Trinity, will repair the damage done by original sin. He is willing to become a man and make up for sin. So the Son of God was born into a first-century Jewish family in Israel. And they named him Jesus.

Why Jesus?

The sin of Adam and Eve was very serious because it was against the all-holy God. No ordinary person, who had his or her own sins to make up for, could make up for the sins of the entire world. The Redeemer had to be sinless, someone equal to God. On the other hand, since human beings committed original sin, a human had to redeem the race. Therefore, atoning for sin required a God-Man, namely Jesus.

A Catholic VIP

St. Ignatius of Loyola
(1491–1556)

St. Ignatius was a soldier from a noble family in Spain. In one battle his legs were injured. While recovering, Ignatius read the life of Christ and a book on saints. These led him to prayer. He hung up his sword and began to write the *Spiritual Exercises*, a prayer guide for Christians. Then Ignatius returned to school to study theology. At the University of Paris, he formed a religious community that vowed to serve the pope. Today they are the Society of Jesus, or Jesuits. The feast day of St. Ignatius is July 31. His motto is "For the greater glory of God."

Name that is above every name

God saves

JESUS

EMMANUEL
God with us

Did You Know?

Another name for Jesus is Emmanuel, which means "God with us."

Jesus

Names have meanings. Andrew means "courageous." Kathleen means "pure." God chose the name Jesus for the God-Man and told his mother, Mary, to call him that. Jesus means "God saves." This is very fitting because "God" is who Jesus is, and "saves" is Jesus's mission.

A name stands for the person. *Jesus*, then, is a holy name. St. Paul says it is "the name that is above every name" and that "at the name of Jesus every knee should bend, in heaven and on earth and under the earth" (Phil 2:9–10). Just saying *Jesus* is a prayer.

Christ

You might think that Christ is the last name of Jesus. It's not. Christ is a title like those we read about in history, such as William the Conqueror or Catherine the Great. It tells about who Jesus is. The word *Christ* is Greek for the Hebrew word *Messiah*, which means "the Anointed One." To be **anointed** means to be set apart for a certain task by being marked with oil. The Jewish people anointed their kings, priests, and prophets. They looked forward to God sending a special savior to establish his kingdom and make them a mighty nation. They called this savior the Messiah.

BTW

To see images of Jesus and other famous religious art, go to http://mv.vatican.va

CHRIST

MESSIAH the Anointed One

Did You Know?

The Chi-Rho symbol for Jesus is made from the first letters in the Greek word for Christ. They are chi (X) and rho (P).

Brainstorm

What do kings, prophets, and priests do?
How is Jesus a king?
How is he a prophet?
How is he a priest?

Jesus was this Messiah, as angels announced to shepherds. St. Peter also declared it when Jesus asked, "Who do you say I am?" Anointed by the Holy Spirit, Jesus was the savior as well as a king, a priest, and a prophet. However, the Jews expected the Messiah to be a great soldier who would overthrow the Romans who occupied their country and oppressed them. Because the kingdom of Jesus was heavenly, not earthly, he usually asked people not to speak about him as the Messiah.

Son of God

The Jews sometimes referred to angels, themselves, and their kings as "sons of God." This title indicated a close relationship with God. When this title is used for Jesus, it has a much deeper meaning. For Jesus truly is the divine Son of God. He is the only Son of God and above all others. St. Peter once called Jesus "the Son of the living God," and Jesus pointed out that Peter understood this mystery only because God revealed it to him.

Lord

The Jews used the word *Lord* for God. By calling Jesus the Lord, we Christians are claiming that he is God. Jesus has the same power, honor, and glory as God the Father. While on earth, Jesus showed this by works of power: calming storms, healing people, raising the dead, expelling devils, and forgiving sins. Jesus is Lord of the world and Lord of history. It's through the Holy Spirit that we say, "Jesus is Lord." In the Bible's last book, Jesus is riding a horse. On his robe and on his thigh this is written: *King of kings and Lord of lords* (cf. Rev 19:16).

BTW

We celebrate the feast of Christ the King on the last Sunday of the Church year.

Scripture Link

A Cure in Jesus's Name

One day after Jesus had returned to heaven, Peter and John went to the Temple. A lame man was being carried to the gate so that he could beg there. When he saw Peter and John, the man asked for money. Peter said, "Look at us. I have no silver or gold, but what I have I give you; in the name of Jesus Christ of Nazareth, stand up and walk." Peter took the man by the hand. At once the man's feet became strong. He jumped up and began to walk. He entered the Temple with the apostles, walking and leaping and praising God. People who recognized him were amazed.

(cf. Acts 3:1–10)

Jesus, Son of God, have mercy on me, a sinner

From My Heart

The ancient "Jesus Prayer" is usually prayed over and over. Pray it now. You might make a habit of praying it.

*Jesus,
Son of God,
have mercy
on me,
a sinner.*

Now Act!

Read Philippians 2:5–11 to learn what Saint Paul said about Jesus. Then ask people you know what role Jesus plays in their lives.

Recap

- Jesus, the Second Person of the Trinity, became a man to save us.

- Jesus is the Messiah, or the anointed one, whom the Jewish people awaited.

- Jesus is Lord and God and has the power of God.

9

How Did God Become Man?

Catechism *Jesus began life as a human being in the Virgin Mary's womb by the power of the Holy Spirit (cf. no. 504).*

What is your favorite Christmas carol? Hundreds of songs have been written to celebrate a great mystery of our faith: the Incarnation. *Carne* means "flesh." The **Incarnation** means that almighty God, who is spirit, becomes a human being, who is both body (flesh) and spirit. God the Son became a man named Jesus, who grew and got tired and hungry, who had human feelings and thoughts. What a wonderful mystery!

God became like us in everything but sin. Why? Because he has tremendous love for us. The Bible says, "God so loved the world that he gave his only Son, so that everyone who believes in him may not perish but may have eternal life" (Jn 3:16). Jesus made up for all sin. Because of him, now we can become sons and daughters of God. We can share divine life.

Jesus, the God-Man

Jesus wasn't part God and part man. He was truly God and, at the same time, truly human. This is a mystery we can't fully understand. Because we can't understand it, people have often held wrong ideas about Jesus. Religious teachings that contradict what the Church teaches are called **heresies** (HAIR-uh-sees). One heresy said that Jesus was not really human. Another taught that Jesus was just a good human who was adopted by God. The Church teaches that Jesus is one divine person, the Son of God, and he has both a divine nature and a human nature. And this means that Mary, the mother of Jesus, is actually the mother of God.

Did You Know?

The Sacred Heart is a symbol of the love Jesus has for the Father and for us.

BTW

According to tradition, the parents of Mary were St. Joachim and St. Anne.

The Annunciation

Sent by God, the Angel Gabriel appeared to Mary, a Jewish girl of Nazareth. After greeting Mary, Gabriel told her that God had chosen her to bear a son whom she was to name Jesus. Her child would be the Son of the Most High and rule an everlasting kingdom. Mary was engaged to Joseph, but they weren't married yet. Gabriel explained that the Holy Spirit would come to her, and her child would be the Son of God. Gabriel also let Mary know that her elderly cousin Elizabeth was six months pregnant with a son. He said that nothing is impossible with God.

Mary answered, "Here am I, the servant of the Lord. Let what you have said be done." With Mary's yes, Jesus miraculously began to form within her. He grew and developed just as you did in your mother's womb before your birth. When Joseph learned that Mary was pregnant, he intended to break off their engagement. But then an angel revealed to him that Mary's child was from the Holy Spirit and would be the Savior. Mary and Joseph were the two holy people God trusted to raise his Son (cf. Lk 1:26–38).

A Loving Visit

Mary traveled to assist Elizabeth until she gave birth to her son, John the Baptist. When Elizabeth saw Mary, the Holy Spirit let her know Mary's secret. Elizabeth exclaimed, "Blessed are you among women and blessed is the fruit of your womb!" Mary sang a prayer, praising God for keeping his promise of a Savior. In this prayer Mary says that all generations will call her blessed (cf. Lk 1:39–56).

A Catholic VIP

St. Joseph (First century)

St. Joseph, the husband of Mary and foster father of Jesus, was known as a good and holy man. He was a carpenter and taught Jesus his trade. Whenever God asked Joseph to do something, he obeyed, even if he didn't understand. According to tradition, Joseph probably died before Jesus left home to begin his ministry. We ask St. Joseph to pray for us because he is the patron of Canada, of the universal Church, of families, of workers, and of a happy death. He has two feast days: March 19 and May 1.

Did You Know?

Mary's prayer is called the Magnificat. In the Church's official book of daily prayers, the Divine Office, or *Liturgy of the Hours*, the Magnificat is prayed every evening.

BTW

Joseph, the legal father of Jesus, was from the house of King David, the tribe of Judah, as prophecies about the Messiah had foretold.

The Savior's Birth

When Mary returned home, she and Joseph went to Bethlehem for a census. On the day they arrived, the inns were full. Mary gave birth to her baby in a stable and laid him in a manger, an animal feedbox. Angels declared the good news to shepherds and sent them to see the Messiah.

The Holy Spirit had told a good man named Simeon that he wouldn't die until he saw the Messiah. One day the Holy Family went to the Temple to present baby Jesus to God, according to the Law. Guided by the Spirit, Simeon came to the Temple, too. He predicted that Jesus would be a light to the Gentiles and that Mary would suffer. Anna was an elderly prophetess who lived in the Temple. She saw Jesus and praised God for sending the promised Messiah (cf. Lk 2:1–38).

Scripture Link

Flight into Egypt

Magi (MAY-jeye), or wise men, from the East followed a star leading to the newborn king of the Jews. King Herod told them to let him know when they found the new king. At the house where the star stopped, the Magi found Jesus, knelt before him, and gave him gifts. This **epiphany** (i-PIF-uh-nee), or revealing of Jesus to Gentiles, shows that he came for all people. A dream warned the Magi not to go back to Herod. Then an angel told Joseph in a dream to flee to Egypt because Herod wanted to kill Jesus. That night the Holy Family left. Herod ordered his soldiers to kill all infants around Bethlehem. After Herod died, an angel told Joseph in a dream to return to Israel. The Holy Family moved to Nazareth.

(cf. Mt 2:1–23)

Brainstorm

Talk about all the Christmas customs you know. How do they reflect the Christmas story as found in the Gospels? Together choose some of these to help you celebrate the Christmas season.

Jesus as a Youth

When Jesus was twelve, he traveled with his parents to Jerusalem for the feast of Passover. On the way home, Mary and Joseph couldn't find him anywhere, so they returned to the holy city. After three days, they found Jesus in the Temple. He was amazing the teachers with his knowledge. Mary asked why he had frightened them by disappearing. Jesus replied, "Did you not know that I must be in my Father's house?" Jesus was referring to the Temple, which was the home of his heavenly Father. Then Jesus went home, obeyed his parents, and grew in wisdom and grace (cf. Lk 2:41–52).

BTW

We celebrate the Feast of the Presentation of the Lord, or Candlemas, on February 2. On that day the candles we use in church all year are blessed in honor of Christ, the Light of the world.

From My Heart

Pray the Hail Mary three times. You can find it on page 231.

Now Act!

Read Mary's prayer, the Magnificat, in Luke 1:46–55. Think of what things you do or have done that praise God.

Recap

· ·

- The Incarnation took place when the Holy Spirit came upon Mary, who was engaged to St. Joseph.

- Jesus is truly God and truly man.

- After Jesus was born in Bethlehem, he was presented in the Temple, where Simeon called him the Light to the Gentiles.

- The Holy Family fled to Egypt to save Jesus from King Herod.

- When Jesus was twelve, he was lost for three days until his parents found him in the Temple, his Father's house.

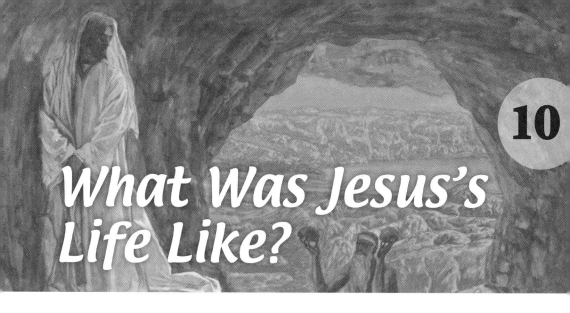

10

What Was Jesus's Life Like?

Catechism *The words and deeds of Jesus as a man revealed that he was God's Son and the redeemer (cf. no. 515).*

What is your favorite name for Jesus—King, Lord, Master, Brother? Jesus is mainly called Son of God and Savior. Everything he did during his public life affirms these two titles. When Jesus was about thirty years old, he left his home, his carpentry business, and Mary to begin his public ministry. For the next three years, Jesus proclaimed the kingdom of God. He was baptized and heard God declare him to be the beloved Son. Before Jesus began his public work, the Holy Spirit sent him to the desert. There for forty days he prepared by praying and fasting.

The Desert Trial

In the desert Jesus was tempted three times by the devil. Satan tempted Jesus to go against his Father's will and not be the kind of Messiah he was sent to be. Jesus resisted the temptations and was faithful to his Father and his mission (cf. Lk 4:1–13).

Prophecies Fulfilled

In a synagogue in Nazareth, Jesus stood up to read from the book of the prophet Isaiah. He read,

"The Spirit of the Lord is upon me,
    because he has anointed me
        to bring good news to the poor.
He has sent me to proclaim release
        to the captives
    and recovery of sight to the blind,
        to let the oppressed go free."

Then Jesus claimed, "Today this scripture has been fulfilled." Jesus was the very Savior the prophets had foretold (cf. Lk 4:16–30).

Did You Know?

Each year during the forty days of Lent we recall the forty days that Jesus spent in the desert praying and fasting. During this time, Satan tried to find out if Jesus was the promised Messiah. The devil tempted him to show off his divine power. Read Luke 4:1–13.

BTW

Jesus wasn't always accepted, even by those who knew him well. The people of Nazareth were once so upset by Jesus's teaching that they tried to throw him off a cliff!
(cf. Lk 4:16–30)

Proclaiming the Kingdom

Jesus announced that God's kingdom was near and that people should be sorry for their sins and believe in the Gospel, the Good News. Jesus would establish the kingdom by his death and resurrection. It would be a kingdom for all nations. The poor, the humble, and repentant sinners would be members. By acting lovingly and accepting Jesus's words, we can enter the kingdom. Jesus taught about the kingdom through stories called **parables**. He also showed signs of the kingdom through his mighty deeds called **miracles**.

The Apostles

Jesus chose twelve men, the apostles, to share his mission. He gave them authority to govern the Church. One day when they were together, Jesus said to Peter, "You are Peter, and on this rock I will build my church." With these words he appointed Peter as leader of the apostles. The apostles and their successors have authority to preach the kingdom and act in Jesus's name (cf. Mt 16:18).

The Transfiguration

Transfiguration (trans-fig-yuh-RAY-shuhn) means "change of appearance." One day Jesus took the apostles Peter, James, and John up a mountain to pray. There Jesus's face and clothes became dazzling with light. Moses and the prophet Elijah appeared and spoke with him. Then a cloud covered Jesus, and a voice said, "This is my Son, the Beloved; listen to him!" The apostles had a glimpse of the glory of Jesus. This vision and the words spoken helped them understand who he was. Their faith was strengthened in preparation for the cruel death of Jesus. Several times Jesus foretold his coming death to the apostles (cf. Mk 9:2–9).

A Catholic VIP

St. Mary Magdalene (First century)

One of the women who followed Jesus was Mary Magdalene. Jesus freed her from evil spirits, and she became his disciple. All the apostles except John deserted Jesus after he was captured. Mary Magdalene, however, was there with John and Mary the Mother of Jesus at the foot of the cross. John's Gospel tells us that after Jesus rose from the dead, he appeared first to Mary Magdalene. He sent her to tell the apostles the Good News that he was alive. So Mary is called "the apostle to the apostles." Her feast day is July 22.

Upsetting the Religious Leaders

Sadducees, scribes, and Pharisees were Jewish leaders. They made sure that the laws and customs of Jewish life and faith were kept. To many of them, Jesus seemed to be a rebel. According to the Law God gave to the Jewish people, no work was to be done on the Sabbath, yet Jesus cured people on that day. No good Jew was supposed to associate with sinners like tax collectors, yet Jesus ate with them and even made one of them, Matthew, an apostle. The Temple in Jerusalem was the holy place where God was present, but Jesus foretold that it would be destroyed. Most importantly, the Jewish faith taught there was only one God, but Jesus spoke of himself as though he were God! He even dared to forgive sins, something that only God has the right to do. Because of this the leaders were unsure of Jesus and so they tested him with many questions and challenges.

Did You Know?

At the Temple in the time of Jesus, the Jews sacrificed animals and produce from their crops to God every day. We understand now that Jesus is the final sacrifice. By his death on the cross, Jesus made himself the perfect sacrifice.

Scripture Link

Jesus Blesses Children

People brought little children to Jesus for him to bless. The apostles scolded the people for bothering Jesus. Instead of thanking the apostles, Jesus was annoyed with them. He said, "Let the little children come to me. The kingdom of God belongs to people who are like children." Then Jesus took the children in his arms and blessed them.

(cf. Mk 10:13–16)

Cleansing of the Temple

In the outer court of the Temple, people sold animals and changed pagan money into Jewish coins. Jesus was angry about the business going on in the sacred place of prayer. He chased out all the merchants. He said, "Stop making my Father's house a marketplace!" Again Jesus revealed himself as the Son of God, but his actions made the leaders of the Jewish people furious (cf. Jn 2:13–23).

Brainstorm

Because it is so many years after Jesus lived on earth, we do not have the opportunity to see him or listen to his voice. How can we know him well today? Where do we hear his teaching? Where can we meet with him?

BTW

Jewish Law is contained in the first five books of the Bible called the Torah. We call these books the Pentateuch (PEN-tuh-took).

From My Heart

Close your eyes and imagine that you have been brought to Jesus. You look into his kind eyes and see his love for you. You sit next to him, and he puts his arm around you. Talk to Jesus and tell him what's in your heart.

Now Act!

Now Act!

Now Act!

Now Act!

Look through a newspaper and find where God's kingdom can be seen today.

Recap

• The Holy Spirit led Jesus to the desert where he was tempted three times.

• Jesus proclaimed the kingdom of God through parables and miracles.

• He chose twelve apostles to share his mission and act in his name.

• Some Jewish leaders became angry when Jesus did such things as drive merchants out of the Temple.

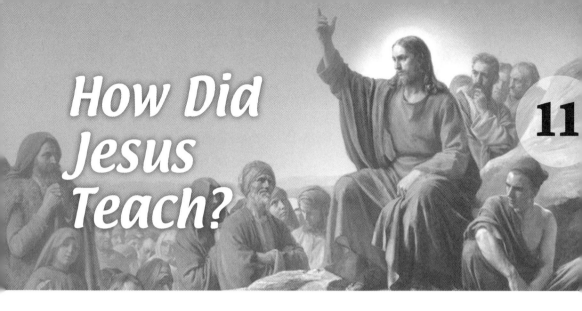

How Did Jesus Teach?

11

Catechism *Jesus taught about the kingdom through parables (cf. no. 546).*

You've probably heard of Aesop's fables. Aesop was a Greek who told stories about animals to teach lessons. Jesus taught by his example, by answering questions, and by preaching. And he also taught through stories. The stories Jesus told are called **parables** (PAIR-uh-buhls). These are stories about people and everyday things that represent something else. Jesus used them to reveal truths about God, God's kingdom, and members of the kingdom. One parable is about a man who sows seed on rocky ground, among thorns, and on rich soil. Only the seed on rich soil yields a large harvest. The seed is like God's word. We, too, can be good soil for the seed of God's word by carefully listening to it (cf. Mt 13:3-9,18-24).

Risk All!

Two parables tell about the value of the kingdom. Jesus spoke of a man who found a treasure hidden in a field. Thrilled, he sold everything he owned to buy that field and have the treasure. Jesus also said that a merchant looking for fine pearls found one that was priceless. He, too, sold all that he had for that pearl. How far are you willing to go when living out your faith? (cf. Mt 13:44–46).

A Catholic VIP

St. Elizabeth Ann Seton (1774–1821)

St. Elizabeth was the first person born in the United States to be named a saint. As a girl in New York, she took food to the poor. She married William Seton, and they had five children. William's business went bankrupt, and he became ill. In hopes of a cure, the couple went to stay with Catholic friends in warm Italy. But William died. Back in the United States, Elizabeth became Catholic. Elizabeth's family and friends didn't understand her choice, and they turned against her. In Maryland, Elizabeth opened the first Catholic school in the country. She also began a religious community, the Daughters of Charity. Her feast day is January 4.

mustard seed

Growth of the Kingdom

In one parable, Jesus compared the kingdom to yeast that a woman put into dough to make it rise. A little yeast goes through all the dough and changes it. Another time, Jesus talked about a small mustard seed that grows into a tree large enough for birds to build their nests in it. The kingdom spreads throughout the world (cf. Mt 13:31–33).

The Wedding Feast

In this parable a king gives a wedding banquet for his son. He sends his servants to tell the people who were invited to come. These people all have excuses for not coming. So the king has his servants go out and bring in everyone they can find. At the banquet, the king sees one guest who doesn't have on a wedding robe. The king has his servants throw this man out.

The wedding feast stands for the kingdom of God. The Jewish people were the first ones invited to the kingdom. With Jesus, God extended his invitation to everyone. The man without the proper clothes is like someone who isn't clothed with grace, God's life, which is needed for the kingdom. We grow in grace through good deeds, prayer, the sacraments, and the work of the Holy Spirit within us. Through grace, we grow in virtue, the habit of doing something good and pleasing to God (cf. Mt 22:1–13).

BTW

Jesus told two parables about how the good and bad live together until the end of time. We must be patient (cf. Mt 13:24–30, 36–43, 47–49).

The Talents

Another parable is about a man going on a journey who gave his servants talents (money) to invest. He gave one five talents, another two talents, and another one talent. When the man returned, the servant with five talents presented him with ten. The servant with two talents gave him four back. The man was pleased with these two servants and promoted them. But the servant who had been given one talent explained that he was afraid of the master and so he hid the talent in the ground. He gave back one coin. The master had him thrown out (cf. Mt 25:14–30). What are you doing with the gifts God has given you? Are you using them for the kingdom?

Did You Know?

Parables are like mirrors in which we see ourselves and like windows through which we see God.

The Good Samaritan

Our expression "a good Samaritan" comes from a parable Jesus told to explain what it means to be a neighbor. Because Jews and Samaritans did not get along, they were suspicious of each other. Jesus said that a traveler was attacked by robbers on the road. They stripped him, beat him, and left him half dead. A Jewish priest came along, saw the victim, and passed by on the other side of the road. Another Jewish leader did the same. But then a Samaritan came near, saw the man, and was moved with pity. He put oil and wine on the beaten man's wounds and bandaged them. He lifted the man onto his own animal and walked him to an inn. There the Samaritan cared for the man all night. The next day he paid the innkeeper and told him to care for the man. He promised to re-pay whatever more was needed. Jesus asked, "Which of the three was a neighbor to the beaten man?" Of course, it's the Samaritan. In other words, all people, even those we don't like, are neighbors to be loved (cf. Lk 10:25–37).

Brainstorm

When we say someone is a good Samaritan, what do we mean? When have you been one? When has someone been one for you?

Scripture Link

Wise Sayings (Book of Proverbs)

∽ "Do not withhold good from those to whom it is due, when it is in your power to do it" (3:27). ∽ "Go to the ant, you lazybones; consider its ways, and be wise" (6:6). ∽ "Fools think their own way is right, but the wise listen to advice" (12:15). ∽ "Whoever walks with the wise becomes wise, but the companion of fools suffers harm" (13:20). ∽ "A soft answer turns away wrath, but a harsh word stirs up anger" (15:1).

From My Heart

The boy Samuel was told to say to God, "Speak, LORD, for your servant is listening" (1 Sam 3:1–11). Repeat Samuel's prayer to tell God you are open to his teachings.

Now Act!

Rewrite one of the parables in this chapter. Set it in modern times.

Recap

- Parables reveal that the kingdom is priceless and that it spreads throughout the world.

- Some parables tell us to answer the invitation to the kingdom by practicing virtue and using our gifts.

- In the parable of the Good Samaritan, Jesus teaches us to love others, even enemies.

How Were Jesus's Miracles Signs of the Kingdom?

12

Catechism

The miracles of Jesus show that the kingdom is in Jesus and that he is the Savior sent by God (cf. no. 547).

When John the Baptist was in prison, he sent his disciples to ask if Jesus was the Messiah. Jesus answered, "Go and tell John what you hear and see: the blind receive their sight, the lame walk, the lepers are cleansed, the deaf hear, the dead are raised, and the poor have good news brought to them" (Mt 11:4–5). Miracles are unexplainable mighty deeds.

Jesus's miracles show his power over evil. The following are the kinds of miracles Jesus worked, each with an example.

Power over Suffering

Several times in Matthew's Gospel we read that Jesus cured all of the sick brought to him. But some accounts of individual healings made their way into the Gospels.

Bartimaeus

As Jesus walked along, Bartimaeus, a blind beggar, called out, "Jesus, Son of David, have mercy on me!" People tried to quiet him, but he called all the louder. Jesus stopped and had the man brought to him. He asked, "What do you want me to do for you?" The man said, "Lord, let me see again." Jesus said, "Receive your sight; your faith has saved you." Just like that, Bartimaeus could see and he followed Jesus (cf. Lk 18:35–43).

Power over Death

At various times Jesus brought the dead back to life. These miracles foreshadowed when he would be raised from the dead and make our resurrection possible. He said, "I am the resurrection and the life. Those who believe in me, even though they die, will live" (Jn 11:25).

BTW

Jesus often worked miracles because people had faith. Sometimes he did them simply out of compassion.

Lazarus

Jesus received word that his friend Lazarus was sick. By the time Jesus arrived, Lazarus had died. Lazarus's sisters Martha and Mary complained that if Jesus had been there, this wouldn't have happened. They were crying, and Jesus wept too. They all went to the tomb, and Jesus ordered, "Take away the stone." Martha warned that Lazarus was dead four days, so it would smell. Jesus prayed and then cried out, "Lazarus, come out!" The dead man walked out alive (cf. Jn 11:1–44).

Brainstorm

When something good happens unexpectedly we say, "It's a miracle!" Sometimes something extraordinary happens, for example, an illness is cured. Why did Jesus work miracles? What miracles do you know of that resulted from people's faith and prayers?

A Catholic VIP

St. Martin de Porres (1579–1639)

St. Martin was born in Peru, the son of a Spanish nobleman and a freed slave. As a barber in those days, he learned remedies for the sick. He joined the Dominicans as a lay member, thinking he was not worthy to take vows as a religious brother. After nine years, his community asked him to become a vowed religious. Martin was in charge of the monastery infirmary and also healed people in the city. Many people thought that his touch alone cured them, but Martin always gave credit to God. He did the lowliest jobs in the monastery and served the poor. St. Martin's feast day is November 3.

Power over the Devil

Jesus resisted temptation himself, and he cast evil spirits out of many people. This showed that he had power to overcome the evil in this world.

The Boy

A man brought his possessed son to Jesus. The boy couldn't speak, and the evil spirit would throw him to the ground where he would lay motionless. He would fall into fire and water. Seeing Jesus, the evil spirit made the boy fall, go into convulsions, and roll on the ground. Jesus said, "All things can be done for the one who believes." The father cried out, "I believe; help my unbelief!" Then Jesus commanded the spirit to leave, and it did (cf. Mk 9:14–29).

Did You Know?

People who had the disease of leprosy were called "lepers." Because leprosy is very contagious, people with the disease were forced to live apart from everyone else and warn people of their approach. Today, leprosy is known as Hansen's disease. With early detection and proper treatment people with leprosy can continue with their normal activities.

Power over Nature

Because God made the laws of nature, God can suspend them. Jesus changed water into wine, multiplied bread and fish to feed a crowd, walked on water, and calmed storms.

Calming a Storm

One night Jesus and the apostles were in a boat when a great storm arose. Waves were swamping the boat, but Jesus was sound asleep. The apostles woke him, saying, "Do you not care that we are perishing?" Jesus calmed the wind and told the sea, "Peace! Be still!" There was dead calm. He asked the apostles, "Why are you afraid? Have you still no faith?" They wondered who this was that even the wind and sea obeyed him (cf. Mk 4:37–41).

BTW

When Jesus sent his disciples out two by two to proclaim the kingdom, they also performed miracles in his name (cf. Lk 10:1–12, 17–20).

Scripture Link

Cure of a Leper

A leper came to Jesus, knelt before him, and said, "Lord, if you choose you can make me clean." Without fear, Jesus touched the leper and said, "I do choose. Be made clean!" Immediately the leprosy was gone. Then Jesus told the man to show himself to the priest and offer a sacrifice. This was what healed lepers had to do according to the Jewish law.

(cf. Mt 8:1–4)

From My Heart

Do you or someone you know need God's healing? Through prayer, go to Jesus for help, just like people did when he lived on earth.

Now Act!

Read these miracle accounts:
The Deaf Man (Mk 7:31-37),
The Paralytic (Lk 5:17–26),
The Gerasene Demoniac (Lk 8:26–39),
and Walking on Water (Mt 14:22–33).
Prepare a news report on one of the cures.

Recap

- **The miracles of Jesus testify that he is the Messiah.**

- **The mighty deeds Jesus worked showed his power over suffering, death, evil, and nature.**

- **Jesus worked miracles as proof of his claims, because of someone's faith, or simply out of compassion.**

13

Why Did Jesus Die?

Catechism *Jesus sacrificed his life by his own free will in order to save us (cf. no. 621).*

Which of these statements do you think is true?

- Jesus struggled with death just as we do.
- People chose to free a murderer rather than to free Jesus.
- After being whipped, Jesus was too weak to carry his cross himself.
- The crime posted above Jesus's head was that he was king of the Jews.
- His mother, Mary, watched him die.

According to the Gospels, all of the above statements about the death of Jesus are true. It is also true that the means of his execution, the cross, has become the symbol for Christianity. We set it atop our churches and wear it around our necks. Because the cross of Jesus brought us life, it is no longer a sign of death but a sign of victory.

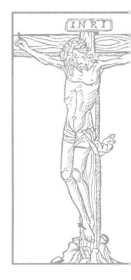

Sign of Love

On the cross Jesus extended his arms to show us how much he loves us. He loved us to death. By dying, Jesus **atoned**, or made up for, all sin: original sin and all our personal sins.

71

Sin shattered our friendship with God, but Jesus repaired it. Now we can be "at one" with God again. God the Father sent his Son for this purpose, and the Son willingly came. Through the Holy Spirit, the salvation of every single person was won. It is our choice to cooperate with God's gift.

A Catholic VIP

St. John (First century)

John and his brother James were fishermen called to be apostles. John, along with Peter and James, was invited to be with Jesus at the raising of Jairus's daughter, the Transfiguration, and the agony (suffering) in the garden. On the cross, Jesus entrusted his mother, Mary, to John. It's thought that John was the youngest apostle, the only unmarried one, and the only one not martyred. He is given credit for writing the Gospel of John, three letters, and the book of Revelation. St. John's feast day is December 27.

The Lamb of God

On the night the Israelites escaped slavery in Egypt, God asked them to sacrifice a lamb and eat it and mark their doors with its blood. That night death came to the firstborn in families, but it passed over the houses marked by the blood. Each year Jews celebrate this Passover meal, the Seder, in a feast called Pasch (pask). Jesus offered himself as our lamb. By his blood we are saved. The mystery of his suffering, death, resurrection, and ascension is the **paschal mystery** (cf. Ex 11:1–13:10).

A Holy Week

Some of the Jewish leaders wanted to get rid of Jesus because he seemed to act against what they believed. Jesus went to Jerusalem for Passover. Despite the danger, he entered the city riding a donkey, and people hailed him as their king. But the apostle Judas accepted thirty pieces of silver from the Jewish leaders to betray Jesus.

That week Jesus ate a Passover meal with his apostles. At the meal he took bread and declared it was his body given for us. Then he took wine and said it was his blood poured out for the forgiveness of sin. In this Last Supper, Jesus offered himself to the Father for us. He established a **New Covenant** (cf. Mk 14:10–25).

Did You Know?

Every year at the end of Lent we recall and pray about the saving acts of Jesus during the **Triduum** (TRID-oo-uhm): Holy Thursday, Good Friday, Holy Saturday, which lead to the great celebration of Easter Sunday.

BTW

To see many forms of crosses, go to http://kids.britannica.com/eb/art-66035.

Did You Know?

Slaves could be freed if someone paid for them. The slaves were said to be ransomed or redeemed. Because Jesus ransomed us from slavery to sin by his death, we call him the Redeemer.

The Suffering of Jesus

After the meal, Jesus and the apostles went to a garden on the Mount of Olives. Jesus asked the apostles to pray, and he went on further by himself, filled with sorrow. He prayed, "Father . . . remove this cup from me; yet, not my will but yours be done." The apostles were sleeping. Then Judas and a crowd arrived. Judas kissed Jesus, and soldiers captured him. A night of suffering followed. Jesus was tried before Jewish leaders and then taken to Pontius Pilate, the Roman governor. Jesus was accused of making himself a king. Soldiers viciously whipped Jesus and mocked him. They put a red cloak on him and pressed a crown of thorns on his head. Pilate asked the crowd to choose to free Jesus or Barabbas, a criminal. They chose Barabbas. Then Pilate ordered that Jesus be crucified. Jesus carried his cross up Mount Calvary, helped by a man named Simon who was passing by (cf. Lk 22:39–23:26).

The Death of Jesus

On Calvary, Roman soldiers nailed Jesus's hands and feet to the cross. They set the cross in a hole between two crucified thieves. Over Jesus's head was posted "Jesus of Nazareth, king of the Jews." The soldiers gambled for his clothes. For three hours Jesus hung on the cross while people mocked him. Mary, the apostle John, and some women stood watching. The other apostles had run away. Peter had even denied knowing Jesus three times (Jn 18:15–18, 25–27). Jesus entrusted Mary to John, saying, "Behold your mother" (Jn 19:27). By saying this, Jesus was giving us Mary as our mother, too. One thief asked Jesus to remember him in his kingdom, and Jesus promised him paradise that day. Finally, Jesus cried out, "Father, into your hands I commend my spirit," and died. Joseph of Arimathea took the body of Jesus down from the cross and buried it in a new tomb (cf. Lk 23:42–43, 46, 50–53).

Brainstorm

What does Jesus's willingness to suffer and die tell you about God? How might you connect your suffering with the suffering of Jesus?

Scripture Link

The Bronze Serpent

During the Exodus, the Israelites had little food and water in the desert. They spoke against God and Moses. So poisonous snakes came and bit the Israelites, who then died. The people admitted to Moses that they had sinned by complaining. They asked him to pray for them. When Moses did, God told him to make a model of a serpent and set it on a pole. Moses made a bronze serpent and put it on a pole. Anyone bitten could look at it and live. As Christians we look to Jesus raised on the cross as the Lord of Life who rescued us from death.

(cf. Num 21:1–9)

BTW

Have you ever noticed the symbol on many ambulances is a serpent twisted around a pole, just like in the story of the bronze serpent (cf. Num 21:1–9)? It is the symbol of the healing profession.

From My Heart

Stations of the Cross are fourteen crosses above pictures or statues placed around a church and used to help us pray about Jesus's death. (See page 239.) Pray what we say at each station:

We adore you, O Christ,
and we bless you, because
by your holy cross you have
redeemed the world.

Develop a habit of making the sign of the cross. What are moments in your day when it would be an appropriate prayer? Do you have a place to keep holy water in your home?

Recap

- **By dying on the cross Jesus made up for all sin and repaired our relationship with God.**

- **Just as a sacrificed lamb saved the Israelites in Egypt, Jesus, the Lamb of God, saved us from eternal death.**

- **At the Last Supper, Jesus offered himself to the Father for us and established a New Covenant.**

What Does Jesus's Resurrection Mean?

14

Catechism *By rising from the dead, Jesus made it possible for us to have new, eternal life (cf. no. 654).*

On Easter we decorate our churches and homes with lilies. Easter lilies symbolize Jesus's resurrection in many ways. They grow in the spring, the season of new life. They are shaped like trumpets, announcing, "He is risen!" They are white, the color of purity. Inside are stamens of gold, a royal color. Like most flowers, lilies begin as a bulb or seed buried in the ground. They burst forth with a new kind of life. This is like Jesus who was buried and then came forth with new, glorious life on Easter morning. He himself referred to this mystery, saying, "Unless a grain of wheat falls into the earth and dies, it remains just a single grain; but if it dies, it bears much fruit" (Jn 12:24).

The paschal mystery of the death and resurrection of Jesus that we celebrate at Easter is the heart of our faith. Because Jesus rose from the dead as he said he would, we know that everything else he said must be true. We know that he is the Son of God. And we know that we too can share in divine life: grace in this world and everlasting life in heaven.

Did You Know?

Before Jesus rose, he went to the place of the dead and freed all people who had been faithful to God, like Abraham and Moses. We profess this belief in the Apostles' Creed.

Jesus's New Life

No one actually saw Jesus rise from the dead, but witnesses saw his burial clothes left in the empty tomb. And later people saw Jesus himself. Jesus didn't rise like Lazarus and the daughter of Jairus. They both had to die again later. Jesus rose with an entirely different kind of life, a new and eternal life. Yet his glorified body still bore the wounds from his death.

The Discovery

The Gospels have varying accounts of how the resurrection of Jesus was discovered. We are told that women went to the tomb with spices to anoint his body. They saw the stone before the entrance was rolled away. Angels told them that Jesus had risen and sent them to tell the apostles. Jesus himself appeared to the women and also sent them to the apostles. Although the apostles didn't believe the women, Peter and John ran to the tomb and saw for themselves that it was empty.

In John's Gospel (20:11–18) Mary Magdalene alone finds the empty tomb. Thinking someone has stolen the body, she cries. A man whom she thinks is the gardener asks why she is crying. As soon as he says her name, Mary recognizes that he is Jesus. He sends her to tell the apostles the good news, and Peter and John run to the tomb (cf. Mt 28; Mk 16; Lk 24; Jn 20–21).

Appearance to the Apostles

On Easter night, the apostles were hiding for fear of being captured. Despite the locked doors, Jesus entered the room. He greeted the apostles, "Peace be with you." Assuming he was a ghost, the apostles were terrified. Jesus showed them his wounds and asked for something to eat to prove he was really alive. Then he breathed on them, saying, "Receive the Holy Spirit," and gave them the power to forgive sins. Thomas, who was absent, doubted what the others told him, so Jesus returned and invited him to touch

Brainstorm

In our Easter celebrations we use many symbols such as butterflies, eggs, and rabbits. Can you explain why these are good symbols of the resurrection of Jesus? Perhaps you can think of other symbols for Easter. How about symbols for heaven?

A Catholic VIP

St. Stephen (First century)

When help was needed, the Holy Spirit guided the apostles to appoint seven good men as deacons. One of them was Stephen. He worked miracles in the name of Jesus and preached well, but some people accused him of speaking against God and Moses. At his trial Stephen had a vision of the glory of God and Jesus standing at God's right hand. Despite this, Stephen was dragged outside the city and stoned. Before he died, Stephen prayed, "Lord Jesus, receive my spirit," and cried out, "Lord, do not hold this sin against them" (Acts 7:59–60). His feast day is December 26.

his wounds (cf. Jn 20:19–27). Later Jesus appeared when seven apostles were fishing and helped them find fish. Then he served them the breakfast he had cooked (cf. Jn 21:4–14). Our faith is founded on the fact that the apostles witnessed that Jesus is alive.

Other Appearances

On Easter day, two disciples walking to Emmaus were joined by a stranger. They told him they were depressed because the one they thought was the Messiah had been killed. The stranger, who was Jesus, explained Scriptures to them and then joined them for dinner. When he broke bread and gave it to them, the disciples realized who he was, and he disappeared. The travelers went back to Jerusalem and told the apostles. The apostles told them that Jesus had also appeared to Peter. Later, in one of his letters, St. Paul wrote that the risen Jesus appeared to more than five hundred people at one time (cf. Lk 24:13–35; 1 Cor 15:1–8).

Did You Know?

In the Holy Land you can visit the Basilica of the Holy Sepulchre (grave) that is built over the places traditionally believed to be Calvary and Jesus's tomb.

The Ascension

After forty days, Jesus commissioned the apostles to go forth and spread the Good News. Then he returned to his Father in heaven. Now he is there in glory at his Father's right hand, a place of honor. His kingdom has begun, and we hope to join him in heaven someday. There Jesus intercedes for us, the members of his body, the Church (cf. Acts 1:1–9).

BTW

"Alleluia" is a Hebrew word that means "Praise the Lord." We sing it especially at Easter. Saint Augustine said that a Christian should be an alleluia from head to toe.

Through us Jesus still lives and acts in the world today. At a time unknown to us, Jesus will return to the world in triumph. At that second coming he will judge all people and God's kingdom will be fully established (cf. 1 Thess 4:13–18).

Scripture Link

St. Paul's Conversion

Saul was a first-century Jew who captured and imprisoned followers of Jesus. One day on his way to Damascus, where there was a Christian community, a light surrounded Saul and he fell to the ground. He heard, "Saul, Saul, why are you persecuting me?" Saul asked, "Who are you, Lord?" Jesus replied, "I am Jesus of Nazareth whom you are persecuting." Jesus told Saul to go to Damascus and he would be told what to do. Blinded by the light, Saul was led to the city. There Ananias was sent by God to cure him. Ananias foretold that Saul would be God's witness to the whole world. We know Saul by his Roman name, Paul.

(cf. Acts 22:3–16)

From My Heart

St. Augustine said that whoever sings well prays twice. Sing "Alleluia" or a song with *alleluias* in it.

Now Act!

Show you have the Easter joy of a Christian in your heart by trying to be cheerful today, even when it is difficult.

Recap

- After dying, Jesus rose with new life.

- The Gospels have several accounts of Jesus appearing to the apostles and others.

- Jesus ascended, that is, he returned to his Father in heaven, where he intercedes for us.

- Jesus will come again to judge all people.

Who Is the Holy Spirit?

15

Catechism *The Holy Spirit is God, equal to the Father and the Son, united with them, and sent to us (cf. no. 689).*

Take a deep breath. Now exhale. By breathing you take in the oxygen that keeps your cells alive and expel waste, carbon dioxide. Not breathing is a sign that a person is dead. The name of the Third Person of the Trinity, Holy Spirit, comes from *ruah*, the Hebrew word for "breath" or "wind." God's breath brought Adam to life. The Holy Spirit is our source of life.

New Knowledge

The Holy Spirit has been at work eternally with the other divine Persons of the Blessed Trinity. Yet the Holy Spirit was the last of the divine Persons to be revealed to us. Hinted at in the Old Testament, the Holy Spirit is promised by Jesus at the Last Supper. The apostles received the Holy Spirit when Jesus appeared to them after his resurrection and breathed on them.

Did You Know?

Pentecost is known as the birthday of the Church. We celebrate it fifty days after Easter.

Pentecost

The Holy Spirit was poured out on the Church fifty days after Jesus rose. The apostles and Mary were together praying on the Jewish feast of Pentecost, a harvest feast. Suddenly loud wind rushed through the house and a flame settled over each person's head. All were filled with the Holy Spirit and began to speak in other languages. The fearful apostles were transformed into bold preachers. They went out and spoke to the crowds. Although people were from different lands, they could all understand the apostles. Peter gave a sermon about Jesus. About three thousand people were baptized that day and received the Holy Spirit. When we are baptized, the Holy Spirit comes to dwell in us too (cf. Acts 2:1–41).

BTW

The Acts of the Apostles is sometimes called the "Gospel of the Holy Spirit" because it shows the Spirit at work in the Church.

The Holy Spirit in Action

If you have faith, that's the Holy Spirit working in you. Scripture says, "No one can say, 'Jesus is Lord' except by the Holy Spirit" (1 Cor 12:3). When you have the urge to pray or do a good deed, that's the Holy Spirit prompting you. Jesus said that his Spirit would be our **paraclete** (PAIR-uh-kleet) or advocate and comforter, someone who is at our side to help us. He said that the Holy Spirit would teach us everything, guide us to truth, and witness to him. Here are some of the ways that the Holy Spirit works in the Church:

- Inspires Scripture
- Guides Tradition
- Assists the teaching authority of the Church
- Puts us in communion with Jesus through prayer and the sacraments
- Causes and supports the good works of the Church
- Makes us holy
- Intercedes for us

A Catholic VIP

St. Catherine of Siena (1347–1380)

Catherine refused to marry and was always praying. This irked her parents until her father saw a dove hovering over her as she prayed. He then realized that Catherine had a special relationship with God. Catherine became a Dominican associate and left her home only for Mass. She sometimes had visions—even one in which Jesus took her as his bride. After three years Jesus sent her out to serve people. She cared for the sick and poor, and was a spiritual mother to many followers. She worked for renewal, for peace, and for the pope's return to Rome from France. St. Catherine is a doctor of the Church. Her feast day is April 29.

Did You Know?

The sun makes crystal shine brightly. The Holy Spirit in us makes us beam love.

Symbols of the Holy Spirit

Because at Jesus's Baptism the Holy Spirit appeared like a dove, artists represent him that way. Wind is another symbol for him based on the name "Spirit" and on the wind of Pentecost. The fire that was seen over the heads of the disciples at Pentecost is also a good symbol of the Spirit because it stands for energy that can change us. Other symbols for the Spirit are a cloud, light, water, and oil. Other names for the Spirit are the breath of God and the finger of God's right hand.

Brainstorm

What examples can you give of people demonstrating a fruit of the Holy Spirit?

Fruits of the Holy Spirit

Through the Holy Spirit we receive God's love and sin is forgiven. The Holy Spirit renews our hearts and transforms creation. We become God's children who have the hope of eternal life. At Baptism the Holy Spirit gives us seven special gifts that he deepens at Confirmation. (You'll learn about them in Chapter 22.) When the power of the Holy Spirit is present in us, we show the good qualities known as the **fruits of the Holy Spirit** (cf. Gal 5 and CCC no. 1832).

Fruits of the Holy Spirit

charity	kindness	faithfulness
joy	goodness	modesty
peace	generosity	self-control
patience	gentleness	chastity

One Mission of Love

The Father, Jesus, and the Holy Spirit are bound together. The Father sent his Son when the Holy Spirit came to Mary. The Spirit also anointed Jesus to carry out his mission. After Jesus rose, he breathed on the apostles and said, "Receive the Holy Spirit" (Jn 20:22). He sent them forth in the Holy Spirit to lead the Church. Now the Spirit of Jesus is alive in the Church, making us children of the Father.

BTW

In the early Church, tabernacles were shaped like a dove.

Scripture Link

Visit from Nicodemus

Nicodemus, a Jewish leader, came to Jesus at night. Jesus told him that no one can see the kingdom of God without being born from above. Nicodemus asked, "How can someone old be born?" And Jesus replied, "No one can enter the kingdom of God without being born of water and Spirit. What is born of the flesh is flesh, and what is born of the Spirit is spirit." He then compared being born of the Spirit to wind that blows where it will and no one knows where it comes from or where it's going. This new birth is Baptism, when we are born of water and the Spirit.

(cf. Jn 3:1–8)

From My Heart

Breathe into me,
Holy Spirit, that my
thoughts may all be holy.
Act in me, Holy Spirit,
that my work too may be holy.
Draw my heart to you, Holy Spirit,
that I may love only what is holy.
Strengthen me, Holy Spirit, to defend
all that is holy. Guard me, Holy Spirit,
that I may always be holy.
—St. Augustine
of Hippo

NOW ACT!

Choose one fruit of the
Holy Spirit and try to show it
in your life.

Now Act!

Recap

• **The Holy Spirit is the Third Person of the Trinity.**

• **Jesus promised us the Holy Spirit, who came to the Church on Pentecost.**

• **The Holy Spirit is our teacher and guide who makes us holy.**

What Is the Church?

Catechism *The Church is all the People of God, formed by God's word and the Eucharist into the Body of Christ (cf. no. 752).*

What picture comes to mind when you hear the word *Church*? You might envision your parish church building. But a more important meaning of the word is "people." Notice the two letters in the middle of *Church*. Who is the Church? You (U) are (R). The Church is everyone God gathers to be united with him. We become a member of the People of God by faith and Baptism.

History of the Church

God thought of the Church long before it came to be. In the Old Testament, God promised to restore our unity with him, which was lost with original sin (the first sin). Through Abraham, God called a people to be his own. When Jesus came as our Savior, the Church became a reality. Jesus brought the kingdom of God to earth. By dying and rising, Jesus made communion with God possible again through the power of the Holy Spirit. The Church became known publicly at Pentecost.

The People of God

Jesus is not only the founder of the Church, but its head. We share in his roles of priest, prophet, and king. We are priestly people who pray, offer our daily lives to God, and join in the sacrifice of the Eucharist. We are prophets who witness to Jesus and speak God's word to the world. And we are royal people who proudly live the laws of God's kingdom and who serve as Jesus did.

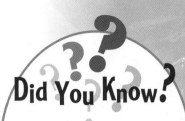

Did You Know?

The pope is the successor of St. Peter and is also the bishop of Rome, the Vicar of Christ on earth, and the Shepherd of the universal Church.

BTW

There are many Christian denominations, such as the Methodists, the Baptists, and the Evangelicals. The efforts made to bring all Christians together as one are what is called the **ecumenical movement**. We pray for Church unity during the Church Unity Octave, January 18–25.

The Body of Christ

What would happen to the branch of a plant if you broke it off? Of course, it would wither and die. Jesus explained that he is like a vine and we are branches (cf. Jn 15:1–8). We share his life. Another image that shows our oneness with Jesus is that of a body. All together we are the Body of Christ, his **Mystical Body**. Jesus is the head, and we are all parts. We are united with Jesus and with everyone else who is united with him. People have different gifts and play different roles in this body, but we are all one. With Christ's help we, his Church, grow to resemble him more and more. The Holy Spirit fills us just as he filled Jesus, making us the temple of God. The Church, then, is divine and human.

Did You Know?

The Church is called the Bride of Christ because he loves her and is one with her.

Marks of the Church

Just as the Trinity is *one*, the Church is one through Jesus and the Holy Spirit. We are united by love, by our shared faith and worship, and by our leaders who have taken the place of the apostles. We must pray and work to preserve this unity.

The Church is *holy* in several ways. Jesus is holy, and we are one with him. Also, we are all called to grow in holiness. Then, too, the goal of the Church is that all may be holy.

The Church is *catholic*, which means universal. In one sense she is catholic because in her is the fullness of Jesus's promise for salvation: the faith, the sacraments, and our leaders. In another sense, the Church is catholic because she is sent to the whole human race. She is missionary, or sent to preach the Gospel to all people for their salvation.

The Church is *apostolic* because she is a spiritual building built on the faith of the apostles; she teaches what the apostles taught, and she is led by the bishops who are the successors of the apostles. What's more, everyone shares in the mission of the apostles to spread the kingdom.

A Catholic VIP

St. Benedict (480?–543)

To live a holy life, Benedict lived in a cave in Italy as a hermit for three years. Men wanted to live as he did, so Benedict began a new form of religious life, the Benedictine Order. His followers, monks, live in an abbey under the direction of an abbot. Women like his twin sister, St. Scholastica, became Benedictine nuns. Benedict wrote a Rule to guide his followers in prayer and in living together. The Benedictine motto is "pray and work." St. Benedict began twelve monasteries. From these, the Benedictines spread over Europe. Their monasteries were centers of learning that helped preserve culture after barbarian invasions. St. Benedict's feast day is July 11.

Church Groups

The **hierarchy** (HY-er-ar-key) is the pope and the bishops called to teach, sanctify, and govern the Church. Priests and deacons are ordained in the sacrament of Holy Orders to assist the bishops. Religious are men and women consecrated to God. Usually they live together in a community, follow their founder's rule, and publicly vow to live the **evangelical** (ee-van-JEL-i-kuhl) **counsels** that Jesus suggested for everyone: poverty, chastity, and obedience. Besides those who join a religious community, other people, such as those who make vows privately, are committed to making themselves and the world holy. The **laity** are Church members who are not ordained or consecrated. Lay people work to spread God's kingdom in the world around them. No matter in what state of life, all God's faithful people have the same mission and the same call to holiness.

> **BTW**
>
> A **charism** is a special grace the Holy Spirit gives to build up the Church for the good of the world. Saint Paul mentions some of these gifts in his letters (cf. Rm 12:6–8 and 1 Cor 12:8–10, 28–30).

> **BTW**
>
> In the United States there are more than 500 religious congregations, such as the Sisters of Notre Dame, the Daughters of St. Paul, the Franciscans, and the Dominicans.

Brainstorm

Learn about missionaries. Some are priests and religious and some are lay persons. Are there concrete ways that you can help them spread the Gospel? What ways can you be a missionary now?

Scripture Link

One Body

St. Paul says, "For just as the body is one and has many members, and all the members of the body, though many, are one body, so it is with Christ. For in the one Spirit we were all baptized into one body." He asks, "If the whole body were an eye, where would the hearing be?" and points out, "The eye cannot say to the hand, 'I have no need of you,'" for the members that seem to be weaker are indispensable. Moreover, "If one member suffers, all suffer together with it; if one member is honored, all rejoice." In the same way, members of Christ's body have different gifts and are one.

(1 Cor 12:12–26)

From My Heart

Do you know the name of the Pope? Who is your local bishop and your parish priest? Does your parish have a deacon? Pray to the Holy Spirit to give them the wisdom and courage to lead us all to holiness and union with God.

Now Act!

Looking through your church bulletin, see if you can find examples of ways that the Church is one, holy, catholic, and apostolic. Think of one way you might be able to be more involved in your parish community.

Recap

• •

- **The Church is the People of God united by faith and Baptism.**

- **Jesus is the founder and head of the Church.**

- **As the mystical Body of Christ, we are united to him and to one another.**

- **The Church is one, holy, catholic, and apostolic.**

- **All Church members—ordained, consecrated, and lay—share Christ's mission.**

What Is the Communion of Saints?

Catechism *God's people, the Communion of Saints, includes those of us on earth, those being purified in purgatory, and the saints in heaven (cf. no. 962).*

Did you ever ask St. Anthony to help you find something? Or pray to St. Jude for an impossible situation? We pray to the saints in heaven because we believe they will help us. But, by the **Communion of Saints** we mean everyone in the Church: those of us on earth who are still alive and struggling to be holy, those in purgatory who have died but must make up for their sins before they can be with God, and those blessed ones in heaven who are already in glory. Besides being a synonym for Church, Communion of Saints can be interpreted to mean the saints' *communion*. Let's first look at this meaning.

Our Communion

We are united, or in communion, in sharing the same holy things: one faith, the sacraments, graces and good works, the goods of the earth, and love. These things draw us together into communion. Above all, we share the Eucharist, which makes us one. When we receive the Body and Blood of Christ, we say we are receiving "holy communion." We are all receiving Jesus and becoming one in him. Because we are bound in unity as the Communion of Saints, whatever good one person does benefits all others. Likewise, whatever evil one person does harms the rest. All of the good that has been done by Church members, plus all the good that Christ did belongs to us all, to the whole Church.

Did You Know?

A candidate for sainthood is called *Servant of God* in the first stage of canonization, *Venerable* in the second stage, and *Blessed* in the third stage before he or she is called *Saint*.

BTW

The three groups in the Communion of Saints are sometimes called Church Triumphant, Church Suffering, and Church Militant. In jest, they are also called All Saints, All Souls, and All Sorts!

Relationships

The people in the Church's three states, like a family, lovingly help one another.

Saints on earth. Did you ever say to someone, "I'll pray for you"? We can pray and offer our good works and sufferings for people on earth, and they can do the same for us.

Saints in purgatory. We can also pray and offer good works and sufferings for people in purgatory in order to hurry their purification. That is why after someone dies, we have Masses said for them. You can pray for your deceased relatives or even for people in purgatory who might not have anyone to pray for them. Those in purgatory (sometimes called poor souls) can also pray for us.

Saints in heaven. Likewise, we can turn to the saints in heaven and ask them to intercede, or pray for us. Friendship with the saints can help us grow closer to Christ.

Heroes and Heroines

The pope adds certain deceased members of the Church to a list (canon) of official saints. This is called **canonization**, which is a long process. First the life and works of a candidate for sainthood are studied in depth to see whether he or she has lived a life of heroic virtue. Unless the candidate is a martyr, two miracles must be attributed to his or her intercession. Finally, the pope declares the person a saint. A great celebration is usually held in St. Peter's Basilica in Rome, and the saint is assigned a feast day. Then the saint may be honored by the Church all over the world. He or she is a model for us, showing us how to become holy by cooperating with the graces of the Holy Spirit and imitating Christ. When we hear about the lives of the saints, our own faith becomes stronger.

Saints are appointed patrons or special supports for countries, people, and causes. For example, St. Stanislaus is the patron of Poland, St. Monica is the patron of mothers, and St. Vincent de Paul is the patron of all charitable works. Churches and Catholic institutions are often named for saints. You might have been given a saint's name when you were baptized. That saint, then, is your **patron saint**. If you don't have one, you can choose one.

A Catholic VIP

St. Andrew Dung-Lac and Companions (died 1820–1862)

Thousands of Catholics suffered during several severe persecutions in Vietnam from 1625 to 1886. One ruler banned foreign missionaries and had them killed. Another vicious persecution was the result of the emperor's suspicion that Christians favored his rebel son. In 1988, 117 martyrs were canonized, a sampling of those who were massacred. The group included a parish priest named Andrew Dung-Lac, eight bishops, forty-nine other priests, and fifty-nine lay Catholics. One martyr was only nine years old. These martyrs together share November 24 as a feast day.

Brainstorm

Find out about your patron saint(s), that is, the patron of your name, your profession (even if you are a student), or of your country. Think of some way to honor them.

Friends in High Places

Saints weren't perfect but had "crooked halos." St. Jerome had a temper, and St. Thérèse was too sensitive. There is a wide variety of saints who show us that holiness is possible no matter what our flaws. They are kings and peasant girls, old women and young boys, popes and parents, teachers, doctors, missionaries, and martyrs. Get to know them now, for with God's grace you will be spending eternity with them!

BTW

A **relic** is part of a saint's body, something the saint wore or used, or something that has touched either of the first two things. The relic is kept in a container called a **reliquary** and is honored by the faithful.

reliquaries

Scripture Link

Praise of the Saints

The Book of Revelation, the last book in the Bible, is a special form of writing called **apocalyptic** (uh-POK-uh-lip-tic). Through symbolic language this book offers hope to Christians who are being persecuted. The book describes the visions of its author, John. At one point he sees heaven. A great multitude of people from every nation stand before God's throne and before the Lamb who is Jesus. They are dressed in white and hold palm branches. They cry out, "Salvation belongs to our God who is seated on the throne, and to the Lamb!"

(cf. Rev 7:9–10)

From My Heart

Find the Litany of Saints on the Internet or in a prayer book and pray it.

Now Act!

Research to learn more about how a saint is canonized. Make a list of all the canonized saints from your country. Use this list as a mini-litany for your personal or familial needs. Invite friends to add their patron saints and the litany will grow.

Recap

• •

- **Church members are in communion by sharing one faith, the sacraments, graces and good works, the goods of the earth, and love.**

- **Church members are united by the Eucharist.**

- **The sacred bread and wine are called Holy Communion.**

- **The Communion of Saints includes people on earth, in purgatory, and in heaven.**

- **Members of the Communion of Saints can pray for one another.**

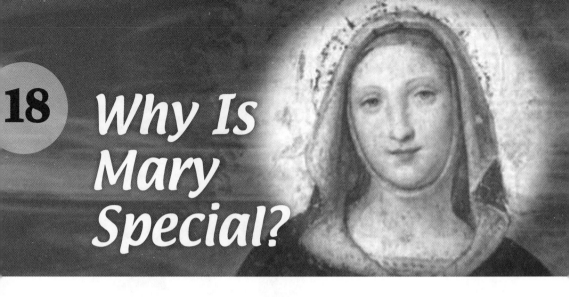

Catechism *The Virgin Mary is the Mother of God and of our Savior as well as the Mother of the Church (cf. no. 963).*

In this monogram for MARIA, can you find all the letters?

Mary is one of the most popular names in the world, and Mary of Nazareth is probably the most famous woman. Out of all the women who ever lived or will live, God chose her to be the mother of his Son, Jesus. Mary is also the mother of Christ's Mystical Body. She is Mother of the Church and our heavenly mother.

Mother of God

Because Mary is God's Mother, God gave her unique graces. From the first moment of her life, she was preserved from original sin, a grace called the **Immaculate Conception**, which means "pure beginning." This is only right. When you give someone a precious gift, you wrap it as beautifully as you can. Jesus is God's best gift to us, so God made Mary as pure and holy as possible. A second grace was the **Virgin Birth**. Mary became pregnant with Jesus by the power of God. No man was involved. Mary was always a virgin. When Mary's life on earth was ended, God took her to heaven body and soul immediately. This grace is called the **Assumption** (uh-SUHMP-shuhn). Mary's assumption foreshadows what awaits all of us. In heaven God made Mary queen over all things.

Did You Know?

These are some special days related to Mary:
Solemnity of Mary, Mother of God, January 1;
Annunciation of the Lord, March 25;
Visitation, May 31; Assumption, August 15;
Birthday, September 8;
Immaculate Conception, December 8;
Our Lady of Guadalupe,
December 12.

BTW

Sometimes Our Lady is called the Immaculate Conception. Under that name, she is patroness of the United States. The beautiful Basilica of the National Shrine of the Immaculate Conception is in Washington, DC. In it are statues of Mary from many countries. www.nationalshrine.com.

Our Mother

If Mary is the Mother of Jesus and we are one with him, then she is a mother to us too. In fact, Jesus gave her as a mother to us when he was dying on the cross. Looking down, he saw Mary and the apostle John. He told Mary, "Woman, here is your son," and he told John, "Here is your mother." John represented us. Jesus was telling us that Mary is our mother. As our mother, Mary loves us and cares for us. Mary was present on Pentecost, the birthday of the Church. She was praying with the apostles when the Holy Spirit came down. More than anything, she wants us to be with her and her son forever in heaven.

Our Model and Intercessor

After Jesus, the Blessed Virgin Mary is the holiest person who ever lived. We call her Queen of All Saints. Mary was the first and best disciple of Jesus. As our heavenly mother, Mary shows us how to live a good life. What does Mother Mary teach us? Above all, Mary had faith. She loved God, listened to him, and did as he wanted. She agreed to be the Mother of Jesus even though she didn't know what would happen. It turned out that she suffered so much that we call her Mother of Sorrows.

Mary also loved others. Although she was pregnant, she went to help her older relative Elizabeth, who also was pregnant. Once, at a wedding, Mary told Jesus the wine was running out. He responded, "What is that to you and me?" Still, Mary said to the servants, "Do whatever he tells you." Jesus changed six jars of water into excellent wine. When we need help, we can turn to Mary and she will pray for us (cf. Lk 1:26–56; Jn 2:1–12).

A Catholic VIP

St. Bernadette (1844–1879)

Bernadette Soubirous (sue-beh-ROO) was from a very poor family in Lourdes, France. She had a hard time studying, and suffered greatly from asthma, but she was good and kind. When Bernadette was fourteen, Mary appeared to her in a grotto, or cave. This was the first of eighteen visits. Our Lady wore a white robe with a blue sash, and she held a rosary, which she prayed with the girl. Then Mary asked Bernadette to have a chapel built so pilgrims could drink from and wash in a spring. Bernadette dug in the ground, and the spring appeared. Mary identified herself as the Immaculate Conception. Each year millions come to Lourdes to pray and to be healed. Bernadette became a religious sister known for her humility. Her feast day is April 16.

BTW

Mary is called the New Eve because new life came to the human race through her.

Devotion to Mary

We adore God alone. When we pray to Mary and the saints, we are not worshiping them. Rather, we are honoring them. God, who made Mary and the saints holy, is pleased. He is especially pleased when we honor his mother, just as you would be pleased if someone honored someone you loved very much. Saturday is Mary's day, and May and October are Mary's months. The best way to honor Mary is to imitate her, for then we will be like Jesus.

A favorite prayer that shows love for Mary is the **Rosary**. This is prayed on a circle of fifty beads in sets of ten called **decades** with a single bead between them. We pray prayers on the beads while we think about Gospel events called **mysteries**. There are four sets of five mysteries, which you'll find on page 237. We begin the Rosary by making the Sign of the Cross with the crucifix. Then we pray an Our Father on the first bead, three Hail Marys on the next three beads, and a Glory Be on the next bead. Before each decade we pause to recall its mystery. Then we pray an Our Father, ten Hail Marys, and a Glory Be. At the end of the five decades, we usually pray the Hail, Holy Queen, which is on page 234.

1. Make the sign of the cross and pray the **Apostles' Creed**.
2. Pray the **Our Father**.
3. Pray 3 **Hail Marys**.
4. Pray the **Glory**, name the first Mystery, and pray the Our Father.
5. Pray 10 **Hail Marys**.
6. Pray the **Glory**, name the second Mystery, and pray the **Our Father**.
7. Repeat steps 5 and 6 until you reach the end.
8. Pray the **Glory** and the **Hail, Holy Queen**. Kiss the crucifix.

Brainstorm

What crosses or sufferings did Mary have in her life that made her Queen of Martyrs? Why do you think Mary is called Mother of Divine Grace? Name three ways you could honor Mary.

Scripture Link

Woman of the Revelation

In *Revelation*, a book of symbols, there is a pregnant woman. She is clothed with the sun, the moon is under her feet, and she has a crown of twelve stars. She gives birth to a son who is to rule all nations. A dragon tries to destroy them but fails. Then it attacks the rest of her children who keep the commandments and witness to Jesus. The woman can stand for Israel or the Church. Catholics also take her to be Mary. Some art depicts the Blessed Virgin with twelve stars around her head.

(cf. Rev 12:1–6, 12–17)

Did You Know?

Mary has appeared on earth, urging us to pray and do penance. She has come as Our Lady of Lourdes, Our Lady of Fatima, Our Lady of Guadalupe, and Our Lady of the Miraculous Medal, among others.

From My Heart

Pray at least one decade of the Rosary for the intention of world peace.

Now Act!
Do research on one of Mary's appearances on earth.

Recap

- Mary, the Mother of God, is the Immaculate Conception.

- God also gave Mary the graces of a virgin birth and the assumption.

- Mary, our heavenly mother, is our model and intercessor.

- We honor Mary when we pray the Rosary.

19 What Will Happen at the End of the World?

Catechism *At the end of the world, Christ will judge all people. The righteous ones, glorified in body and soul, will reign with him forever. The kingdom of God will be fully established (cf. nos. 1040, 1042).*

When we look around at the world and see all of its wonders, it is difficult to imagine that some day it will come to an end. Scripture and science both tell us that this is true. However, it is not something to worry about. Living our lives well and relying on God's grace is what is important. Then at the end of our lives we will go to heaven, which is what we call life with God.

Some people think that heaven is where good people become angels, live on fluffy clouds, and play harps. That doesn't even come close! St. Paul says that we can't even imagine what heaven is like. What we do know about the afterlife comes from the teachings of Jesus and his Church. They tell us about the four last things: death, judgment, heaven, and hell.

Death: A Door

When God created us, he did not plan that we would die. Death is the result of the sin of Adam and Eve. When people we love die, we are sad because we won't see them again on earth. It is sad to know that someday we too will die. But our faith in Jesus gives us hope. Death for us is only a door to another world. By dying, Jesus has made death a way to reach a new and glorious life that will last forever.

Did You Know?

In eternity we will have glorified bodies like the risen Jesus has. We will be beautiful and radiant. We will be able to move quickly wherever we please and be able to pass right through material things as if they weren't there.

A Personal Judgment

At death our soul will be separated from our body. We will meet Christ and be judged as an individual on our faith and our works. Immediately we will realize whether we have grace, God's life, or have separated ourselves from God. This is called the **particular judgment**.

People who by God's grace loved both God and others and who remained friends with God will be rewarded. They will enter heaven. People who seriously sinned and are not sorry, have chosen to separate themselves from God and go to hell. Some people who die in the state of grace still are not worthy to be in God's presence. Perhaps they haven't made up for all their sins. These people gladly undergo purification in **purgatory** (PUR-guh-tor-ee) before entering heaven.

St. Pio of Pietrelcina (1887–1968)

St. Pio (Padre Pio) was the son of peasant farmers in Italy. He joined the Capuchins and became a Franciscan priest. Two years later he offered his life to God in order to help the souls in purgatory. Always in poor health, Padre Pio had much suffering to offer. He is known for his spiritual experiences, especially the **stigmata** (stig-MAH-tuh), which are Christ's wounds appearing on the body. Embarrassed by the painful stigmata, Padre Pio usually covered his hands. Crowds came to his Masses, which could last two hours. People kept him busy in the confessional many hours each day. Padre Pio opened two hospitals, and one was called Home to Relieve Suffering. His feast day is September 23.

Heaven

Heaven is being with God and seeing him in what is known as the **beatific** (bee-uh-TIF-ik) **vision**, which gives us supreme joy. Jesus opened heaven to us. In heaven we will be united not only with Christ, but also with Mary, the angels, and all the other saints. We will be perfectly happy, and this glorious life will last forever.

Purgatory

All who live their lives in friendship with God, but who are not yet ready to enter heaven, pass through purgatory. The people in purgatory know that eventually they will enter heaven. This purification of purgatory, which is like a cleansing fire, makes them holy. Our prayers and good works offered for them can help them complete the journey more quickly.

Hell

Hell is everlasting separation from God. Those who die in mortal (serious) sin have deliberately turned away from God. They refused to love him. We were created for God, and we need him more than anything else. Only with God will we be perfectly happy. Although God wants everyone to be saved, we are free either to accept God's grace and choose to be saved or to reject it. Jesus speaks of hell as fire that never ends. It is like regret. When we regret something, it burns like a fire that cannot be put out.

The Last Judgment

Every so often someone predicts when the end of the world will occur. But Jesus told us that no one knows when the world will end except the Father. At the end of time, all of the dead will be resurrected. Their souls will be reunited with their bodies. Christ will come in glory, and all nations will appear before him. Then all the good that people did or failed to do will be revealed. Christ will judge with divine justice. This second coming of Christ is called the **parousia** (pah-ROO-zee-uh).

Then God's kingdom will come in the perfection God planned. The good will reign forever with Christ and be a community. The whole universe will be transformed. There will be a new heaven and a new earth. Death, crying, and pain will be no more. We will live in peace and love. And God will be "all in all," which means we will be happy with God forever.

BTW

In heaven everyone will be completely happy Each one of us is unique. So our happiness will be uniquely ours. We will be like different sized cups that are each filled to the brim. Each cup holds a different amount, but each one is full.

Brainstorm

How would you explain heaven to someone who has never learned about it? What about purgatory and hell? Who do you look forward to seeing in heaven?

Did You Know?

Jesus compared heaven to a wedding feast (cf. Mt 22:1–14). Also, before Jesus died, he told the apostles, "In my Father's house there are many dwelling places. If it were not so, would I have told you that I go to prepare a place for you?" (Jn 14:2).

Scripture Link

The Judgment of Nations

Jesus said that when the king comes in glory he will separate all people into groups like sheep and goats. He will invite the sheep into heaven, saying, "I was hungry and you gave me food, I was thirsty and you gave me something to drink, I was a stranger and you welcomed me, I was naked and you gave me clothing, I was sick and you took care of me, I was in prison and you visited me." These good people will ask, "When did we do these things?" and the king will answer, "Just as you did it to the least of my brothers and sisters, you did it to me." Then he will send the "goats" away from him to hell because they did not do these things.

(cf. Mt 25:31–46)

BTW

The Book of Revelation ends with the word "Maranatha" (mar-ra-NA-tha), which means "Come, Lord Jesus!"

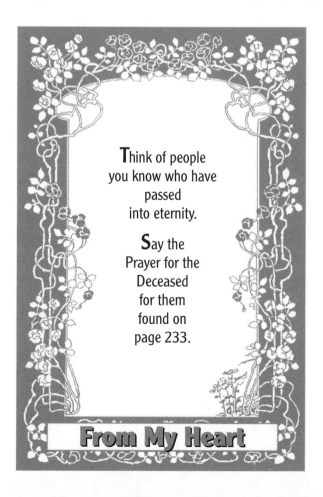

Think of people you know who have passed into eternity.

Say the Prayer for the Deceased for them found on page 233.

From My Heart

Now Act!

Read 1 Corinthians 15:35–57
about the resurrection of the dead.

Recap

• •

- At our death Jesus will judge us in a particular judgment.

- People who haven't made up for their sins are purified in purgatory.

- Heaven is being with God and enjoying perfect happiness.

- Hell is everlasting separation from God.

- Jesus will come to judge everyone at the end of the world.

20 Why Is Liturgy Important?

Catechism *In the liturgy Jesus Christ acts as high priest and continues his saving acts in, with, and through his Church (cf. no. 1069).*

Wouldn't it be great if you could relive a special vacation or an exciting game over and over? But now all that is left is a memory.

The world's most stupendous event was the paschal mystery, that is, the passion, death, resurrection, and ascension of Jesus. Each time Mass is celebrated, this mystery is present again.

The Liturgy

The **liturgy** (LIT-er-jee) is the Church's official public worship. First and foremost it refers to the celebration of the Eucharist. It also includes the other **sacraments**, or rituals in which we meet Christ and receive grace. The word *liturgy* originally meant "a public work" or a service on behalf of the people. For us it means our participation in the work of God. In the liturgy, Christ our priest is acting; but we, his body and a priestly people, are acting, too. Together we are making the world holy.

112

At the liturgy, the Church prays to the Father with Jesus in the Holy Spirit. It is the most sacred action possible. This worship is the life of the Church. Our lives and all our actions are directed by it. At the same time, this worship gives us power to be who God called us to be, and bring salvation in Jesus to others.

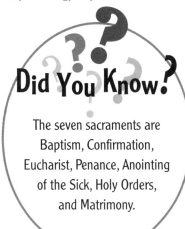

Did You Know?

The seven sacraments are Baptism, Confirmation, Eucharist, Penance, Anointing of the Sick, Holy Orders, and Matrimony.

Christ's Work

Did you ever wish you lived when Jesus did so you could see and hear him? Well, he still speaks and acts in the seven sacraments he gave us. He gives us grace in ways that we can see, hear, feel, smell, and taste. He uses things from everyday life, like water, bread, and oil. The things used and the words said in the sacraments are signs of what is happening in us. More than that, they bring about the grace they signify. For example, the water of Baptism is a sign of God's power to remove original sin, and being baptized really does cleanse the soul of original sin.

The power of the sacraments does not depend on the holiness of the minister or the one receiving the sacrament, but on Christ.

Jesus entrusted the sacraments to the Church through the apostles and their successors. Jesus is present and acting in all the sacraments. Every liturgical action is an encounter between Christ and his Church. In the liturgy we already participate in the eternal liturgy of heaven. With all the saints and angels we glorify God.

BTW

The sacraments match experiences of our natural life: birth (Baptism), growth (Eucharist, Confirmation), healing (Penance, Anointing of the Sick), and mission (Holy Orders, Matrimony).

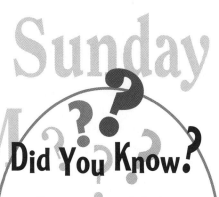

Did You Know?

Sacramentals are holy signs that are related to the sacraments and help us receive grace. They signify effects that are obtained by the prayers of the Church. Some sacramentals are blessings, holy water, rosaries, and medals.

Brainstorm

Besides the feasts of Christmas and Easter, what other feasts of the liturgical year are you familiar with? What could you praise and thank God for at the liturgy on those days?

The Holy Spirit

The Holy Spirit is very active in our liturgy. He prepares us to meet Christ in it. He recalls and makes Christ known to us. The Holy Spirit's power makes Christ's saving work present and active. And finally, he makes the gift of our communion with God bear fruit.

The sacraments strengthen and express faith. Each sacrament gives a special grace called **sacramental grace**. All of the sacraments make us more like Christ, more like God, through the power of the Holy Spirit. They make the Church grow in love and in witnessing to Jesus. But the fruits that the sacraments bear depend on our own attitudes.

Sacred Times and Places

We celebrate the paschal mystery every Sunday, the Lord's Day. In addition, throughout the **liturgical year**, or Church year, we celebrate different aspects of the paschal mystery. This year revolves around the Incarnation and the Redemption. The highpoint is the Easter season, when we remember the resurrection of Jesus. During the year we also observe feasts of Mary and the saints. Our celebrations usually take place in a church. This sacred building is a symbol of us, the living stones of the spiritual temple. It also symbolizes the Father's house, heaven.

The Divine Office

The Divine Office, also called the Liturgy of the Hours, parallels the theme and prayers of the day's Mass. Its seven "hours" prayed throughout the day are chiefly taken from Scripture. Priests and most religious pray the Office, but it is a way for all Christians to make the whole day holy.

BTW

A **rite** is a sacrament's prayers and actions. Catholic rites developed in different places and cultures. Throughout the world, most Catholics follow the Roman rite. Other Catholics celebrate liturgy with rites such as the Byzantine, Coptic, or Maronite.

Did You Know?

The seasons of the liturgical year are Advent, Christmas, Ordinary Time Part I, Lent, Easter, and Ordinary Time Part II.

A Catholic VIP

St. Gregory the Great (540?–604)

Pope Gregory I was the son of a wealthy Roman senator and St. Sylvia. He always had a place in his heart for the poor. For a time Gregory was governor of Rome. He left this position to become a monk and founded six Benedictine monasteries. Gregory was chosen as pope by the people. He called himself servant of the servants of God. As pope, Gregory sent monks to teach the faith in England. He also made peace with the Lombard invaders and restored order in the Church. He is known for reforming the liturgy, and Gregorian chant is named for him. Gregory is a doctor of the Church. The Church still has some of his many writings and homilies. His feast day is September 3.

Scripture Link

Our liturgy is rooted in Jewish liturgy. Psalm 100 tells how to worship.

Make a joyful noise to the LORD, all the earth.
Worship the LORD with gladness;
come into his presence with singing.
Know that the LORD is God.
It is he that made us, and we are his;
we are his people, and the sheep of his pasture.
Enter his gates with thanksgiving,
and his courts with praise.
Give thanks to him, bless his name.
For the LORD is good;
his steadfast love endures forever,
and his faithfulness to all generations.

(Ps 100:1–5)

From My Heart

The liturgy is filled with Scripture. Find a few verses in the Gospel of Mark and read them. Ask yourself, "What is Jesus saying to me through them?"

Now Act!

Make a floor plan of your church. Include the altar, ambo, tabernacle, sanctuary lamp, baptismal font, and paschal candle. Then write how each feature is related to the liturgy.

Recap

- Liturgy is the Church's official public worship in which we pray to the Father with Jesus in the Holy Spirit.

- In the seven sacraments, Jesus acts through things and words that symbolize what he is doing for us.

- Each sacrament gives sacramental grace and makes us more like Christ.

- During the liturgical year we celebrate events in the life of Christ.

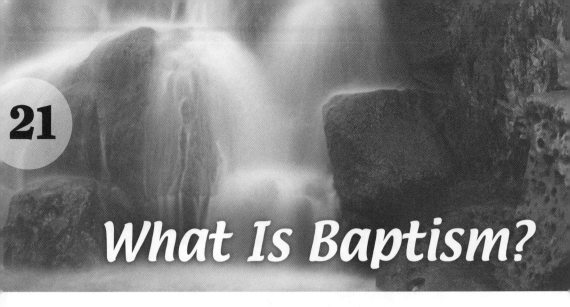

21

What Is Baptism?

Catechism *Baptism is the sacrament through which we are freed from sin, become children of God and members of Christ and his Church, and share in the Church's mission (cf. no. 1213).*

Water has the most variety of uses of any substance. How many can you think of? It also covers three-fourths of the earth's surface and makes up more than half of our bodies. We need water to live. Water, then, is the perfect symbol for Baptism, our first and most necessary sacrament.

Baptism is one of the sacraments of initiation, along with Confirmation and Eucharist. It is an encounter with Christ that unites us with him and makes us a member of the Church. It initiates or begins our relationship with Christ. In Baptism we are reborn. Baptism cleanses us from sin and fills us with the divine life of grace. Through Baptism we can celebrate the other sacraments and, if we live a good and just life, eventually enter the kingdom of God.

What Baptism Means

People who believe in Jesus and want to be his followers are baptized. The apostles baptized people, as Jesus had directed them to do (cf. Mt 28:18–20). The early practice was to have people walk down into a pool and then walk out. This symbolized being united with Christ in his death and rising. After all, it's the paschal mystery that won new life for us. Today some parishes have baptismal pools, but most have fonts.

BTW

The word *Baptism* comes from the Greek word for "plunging" or "immersing."

Did You Know?

Bishops, priests, and deacons are ordinary ministers of Baptism, but in an emergency anyone can baptize by saying the words "I baptize you in the name of the Father and the Son and the Holy Spirit" while pouring water over the person's head.

BTW

We renew our baptismal promises each year at the Easter Vigil.

Adult Initiation

People who wish to be baptized into the Church go through a liturgical experience called the **Rite of Christian Initiation of Adults** or RCIA. They are called **catechumens** (kat-i-KYOO-muhnz). Over a period of time they study the faith and learn how to live it. At each stage the catechumens celebrate a special rite. Finally at the Easter Vigil they celebrate all three sacraments of initiation. This Rite is also adapted for children of a catechetical age.

A Catholic VIP

St. Perpetua and St. Felicity (died 203)

Perpetua, a twenty-two-year-old in Carthage, Africa, had a baby boy. Felicity was her pregnant slave. The two women, who were catechumens, were arrested when Emperor Severus made it a crime to be a Christian. Perpetua kept a record of their sufferings in prison. When her pagan father pressured her to worship pagan gods in order to be freed, she replied, "I cannot be called by any other name than what I am—a Christian." Two days after Felicity gave birth, the women were martyred. They were thrown to a wild beast and eventually killed by a sword in an arena as entertainment for a national holiday. Their feast day is March 7.

The Rite of Baptism

The celebration begins with the Sign of the Cross, the sign of our redemption. The Word of God is proclaimed. Then because Baptism frees us from sin, the celebrant says words of **exorcism** (EK-sor-siz-uhm) so that all evil will be driven out. The celebrant anoints the person with the oil of catechumens. The person then makes baptismal vows, or promises. He or she rejects Satan and confesses the faith of the Church. This faith will grow after Baptism.

The baptismal water is consecrated. The Church prays that the Holy Spirit be sent upon it so that those baptized in it may be born of water and the Spirit. Then the catechumen is baptized. The most common way is by pouring the water three times over the person's head. At the same time the celebrant says, "(*Name*), I baptize you in the name of the Father, and of the Son, and of the Holy Spirit."

Then the person is anointed with chrism, another holy oil. It is a sign of the Holy Spirit who comes to the person. *Christian* means "anointed one." The person is now one with Christ and shares in his role of priest, prophet, and king. The newly baptized is given a white garment as a symbol that he or she has put on Christ and has risen with him. The person also receives a candle lit from the paschal (Easter) candle that stands for Christ. This symbolizes that he or she is now enlightened by Christ to bring light to the world.

Brainstorm

Because we have been baptized, we are true members of Christ's Church.

What are some rights of a Christian?

What are some responsibilities?

Special Graces of Baptism

In Baptism all sins are forgiven (original sin and actual sin) and all punishment due for sin is cancelled. The person is **justified**, or made right with God and is filled with sanctifying grace, God's life. United with Christ, the newly baptized is now an adopted child of God. He or she is a member of Christ, an heir to heaven, and a brother or sister to all other Christians.

At Baptism a person becomes a temple of the Trinity. He or she receives the virtues of faith, hope, and charity as well as the gifts of the Holy Spirit to grow in holiness. Baptism seals a Christian with an indelible spiritual mark (**character**) as belonging to Christ. So this sacrament can only be received once.

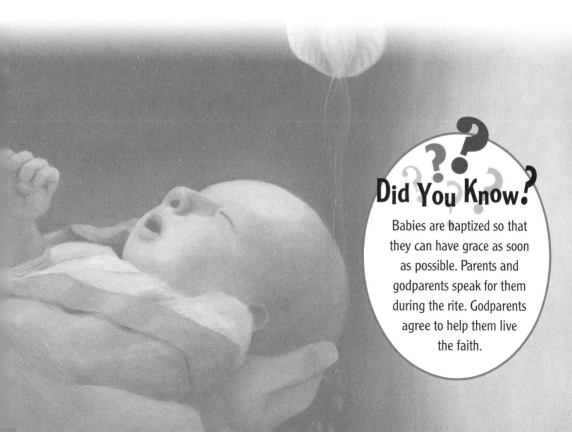

Did You Know?

Babies are baptized so that they can have grace as soon as possible. Parents and godparents speak for them during the rite. Godparents agree to help them live the faith.

Scripture Link

Water in the Exodus

As the Israelites fled from Egypt, they came to the Red Sea. At God's direction, Moses stretched his staff over the sea, and the waters parted. The chosen people walked safely through it. As Pharaoh's army pursued them, the waters flowed back and drowned all the soldiers. At the end of the Exodus, the Israelites came to the Jordan River. It too parted to let them arrive at the Promised Land.

(cf. Ex 14:10–31; Josh 3:14–17)

We can see a comparison with Baptism. In this sacrament through water we are saved from slavery to sin and can reach our promised land of heaven.

From My Heart

Ask Jesus to help you keep your baptismal promises. Then pray the Apostles' Creed on page 232.

Now Act!

Tell someone why you are glad to be (or hope to be) a Catholic. If you've been baptized, write a news article about it. Include the date, the names of the minister, your godparents, the church, your name, patron saint, and the weather. Look at photos. Do you still have your garment and candle?

Recap

• Baptism, the first and most necessary sacrament, cleanses us from sin, unites us to Christ, and makes us children of God and members of Christ and his Church.

• Baptism is carried out by water and words through the power of the Holy Spirit.

• Baptismal promises are a profession of faith and a rejection of sin.

• Baptism leaves an indelible mark and makes it possible for us to celebrate the other sacraments.

• Ordinarily during the Rite of Christian Initiation of Adults (RCIA), all three sacraments of initiation are received.

22

Why Be Confirmed?

Catechism *The sacrament of Confirmation completes the baptismal grace by more perfectly binding the baptized person to the Church and strengthening him or her with the gifts of the Holy Spirit (cf. no. 1285).*

Imagine you are in the upper room on Pentecost morning. You are sitting with Mary and the apostles. Suddenly you hear a noise like a train coming. It's wind roaring throughout the whole house and shaking it. Flames appear in the room. You gasp. The tongues of fire separate and settle, one over each person's head. Everyone starts speaking in different languages. The Holy Spirit has come and filled the Church. (See Acts 2:1-12.)

The same Holy Spirit who came down upon Mary and the apostles in the upper room on Pentecost comes to us in the sacrament of Confirmation. His coming now is not as dramatic as on Pentecost. Instead of in wind and fire, the Holy Spirit comes in the signs of laying on of hands, anointing with oil, and the words, "Be sealed with the Gift of the Holy Spirit." We already received the Holy Spirit at Baptism. But in this second sacrament of initiation the Spirit comes to "confirm" and strengthen what Baptism did for us. Confirmation increases and deepens baptismal grace and gifts.

More Grace, More Responsibility

In Confirmation we are more closely bound to the Church and receive greater strength to live as a Christian. The other side of the coin is that we bear more responsibility for being a witness to Christ. Empowered by the Spirit, the apostles no longer hid in fear but burst forth from the upper room to preach about Jesus. After Confirmation we too have an obligation to spread and defend the faith by word and action.

Did You Know?

Bishops consecrate chrism and the other holy oils for their dioceses at a Chrism Mass on Holy Thursday. There are three holy oils: Holy Chrism, Oil of the Catechumens, and Oil of the Sick. They are kept in a special place in church called an **ambry (AM-bree)**.

Background of Confirmation

Jesus was filled with the Holy Spirit, and he promised this Holy Spirit to his Church. After Pentecost, the apostles in turn passed this special gift of the Holy Spirit to the baptized through the laying on of hands. This act was soon combined with the anointing with **chrism** (KRIZ-uhm), a fragrant oil. This sign is related to Christ, who was anointed by the Holy Spirit. Once we are anointed with oil we are consecrated to share more in the mission of Christ.

Oil is a great symbol for Confirmation. It is a sign of abundance and joy. Moreover, oil is used to cleanse and heal, soothe and strengthen, and to make beautiful.

Brainstorm

Why is oil a good sign for Confirmation?

A Catholic VIP

St. Francis Xavier (1506–1552)

When Francis Xavier from Spain studied at the University of Paris, he was ambitious. He was a good athlete focused on his career. Then a fellow student, St. Ignatius of Loyola, posed to him a question Jesus had asked: "What does it profit a man if he gains the whole world but loses his soul?" (cf. Mt 16:26). So Francis gave up his life of fame and pleasure and joined Ignatius as a Jesuit. Francis became a priest who was very enthusiastic about spreading the Gospel. He sailed to India where he baptized thousands. Then he worked in Malaysia and Japan. But his dream was to bring the Gospel to China. On the way there he became ill. Francis was taken off the ship and left on an island, where he died in sight of China. This missionary is known as the Apostle of the Indies. His feast day is December 3.

Who Receives Confirmation?

All people who are baptized can and should receive Confirmation. We prepare by studying the faith more and by praying more intensely. We learn about Jesus, the Holy Spirit, and what it means to belong to the Church as a whole and as a parish. This preparation makes us better able to carry out our responsibilities as Christians. To be confirmed, people must be in the state of grace. For this reason, candidates prepare for this sacrament by receiving the sacrament of Penance in which sins are forgiven.

BTW

The Eastern Churches call Confirmation "Chrismation."

The Rite of Confirmation

Except when Confirmation occurs right after Baptism, it begins with a renewal of baptismal promises and a profession of faith. Then the bishop extends his hands over the group to be confirmed and prays. He asks the Father to send the Holy Spirit upon them to be their helper and guide. He asks that they be given the seven gifts of the Holy Spirit. Then the bishop confers the sacrament by anointing each person with chrism on the forehead (the laying on of hands). He says, "Be sealed with the Gift of the Holy Spirit." The Rite ends with the sign of peace.

The Mark of Confirmation

A seal makes a document official. Long ago soldiers were marked with their leader's seal. The anointing with chrism marks us with the seal of the Holy Spirit. It means we belong to Christ and share in his mission. Like Baptism, Confirmation gives us an indelible spiritual mark, or character. So it, too, can only be received once.

The Gifts of the Holy Spirit (cf. no. 1303)

Wisdom – I know God's plan, put God first, and see things from his point of view.

Understanding – I have insight into what God revealed.

Counsel – I seek and am open to good advice. I possess right judgment.

Fortitude – I have strength and courage to do what is right even when it's difficult.

Knowledge – I know God and what he expects of me.

Piety – I love and worship God and respect all that God created.

Fear of the Lord (Wonder and awe) – I respond to God's holiness with wonder, humility, and holy respect that keeps me from sinning.

Did You Know?

A Confirmation sponsor is a practicing Catholic who will be a guide and model for the one to be confirmed. It's recommended that the sponsor be one of the person's godparents.

Scripture Link

The Creating Spirit

The Bible opens with the story of creation. When there was nothing but darkness, a mighty wind swept over the waters and God said, "Let there be light." The Hebrew word for wind also means "spirit." At the dawn of creation, we see the power of God bringing forth the universe and life. Today we celebrate the creation of new life in Baptism and Confirmation. When we receive these sacraments, the Holy Spirit comes and fills us with divine life.

(cf. Gen 1:1–3)

From My Heart

Which of the seven gifts do you especially need? Ask the Holy Spirit to increase that gift in you.

Now Act!

For each gift of the Holy Spirit, give an example of someone living it today.

Recap

- In Confirmation, which is ordinarily conferred by a bishop, the Holy Spirit comes to complete the grace of Baptism in us.

- Confirmation gives us more strength to live as a Christian but also increases our responsibility to spread the faith.

- The signs of Confirmation are the laying on of hands, anointing with oil, and the words, "Be sealed with the Gift of the Holy Spirit."

- Confirmation imparts an indelible spiritual mark.

23

Why Is the Eucharist Wonderful?

Catechism *The Eucharist, a memorial of the death and resurrection of Jesus, re-presents his sacrifice. It is a means of Church unity and holiness as we share the sacred Body and Blood of Jesus (cf. no. 1323).*

For people over much of the world, bread is "the staff of life," something their life depends on. Different kinds of flour and added ingredients, such as yeast or salt or eggs, make a wide assortment of bread. But Jesus chose plain bread made only from wheat and water for the third sacrament of initiation, the Eucharist. He also chose grape wine. At Mass, these two elements become the Body and Blood of Jesus. Through the priest's words over the bread and wine, and by the power of the Holy Spirit, Jesus comes to earth. He is wholly present, God and man. The sacred bread and wine keeps his Church alive.

The Last Supper

Jesus instituted the Eucharist on the night before he died. He was eating supper with his apostles at Passover time. During the meal, Jesus took bread, thanked God for it, broke it, and gave it to his apostles. He said, "This is my body. Do this in memory of me." Jesus also took a cup of wine, gave thanks for it, and passed it around. He said, "This is my blood, which is poured out for many for the forgiveness of sin." Jesus made a new covenant between God and us. He offered himself to the Father for us. Ever since then his followers have celebrated the Eucharist, remembering the Lord's death and resurrection. It is our most perfect prayer and the center of our Christian lives (Mt 26:26-28).

Worship

At **Mass**, Catholics gather to worship God together. *Eucharist* means "thanksgiving." At every Mass, we thank and praise God for creating us, for redeeming us, and for making us holy. We also offer sacrifice. Under the forms of bread and wine, Jesus, our high priest, offers himself to the Father. His sacrifice on the cross is made present again, and redemption goes on. This time we join in his offering. We offer Jesus to the Father, and we offer ourselves with him. Our liturgy is one with the liturgy of heaven where angels and saints praise God.

BTW

The changing of the bread and wine into the body and blood of Jesus is called **transubstantiation** (tran-suhb-stan-shee-AY-shuhn). This means that the bread and wine still look very ordinary, but they have truly become the Body and Blood of Jesus.

Did You Know?

The Eucharist is also called the Blessed Sacrament. After Mass, any remaining consecrated hosts are kept in a special place of honor called the **tabernacle** (TAB-er-nak-uhl). From here, Holy Communion can be taken to the sick. We may also adore Jesus in the Blessed Sacrament by visiting him.

Communion

Amazingly, Jesus becomes food for us. When we eat the sacred bread and drink the sacred wine, Jesus is united with us. No union is more complete. You know that your food becomes you. But in Communion we become more like Jesus. And because everyone who receives Communion receives the same Jesus, we are also united with Church members all over the world. We become one body. This is why the Church is called the Body of Christ. Jesus nourishes, strengthens, and unites his Church every day through the eucharistic banquet. Communion is a foretaste of heaven, where we will be united with God and one another forever.

BTW

The table the sacrifice is offered on is an **altar**. The priest wears special clothes called **vestments**: a white robe (**alb**), a band of cloth over his shoulders (**stole**), and a flowing outer garment (**chasuble**). The container for the hosts is a **ciborium**, and the cup for the wine is a **chalice**.

Brainstorm

What are your favorite parts of the Mass? Do you speak to Jesus in your own words as you prepare to receive Communion? How do you pray right after Communion? How would you explain the importance of these moments of personal prayer?

The Mass

The Mass has two main parts: the **Liturgy of the Word** and the **Liturgy of the Eucharist**. Here is an overview of the Rite:

We speak to God. We ask forgiveness for our sins and praise God.

God speaks to us. We listen to Scripture readings. Before the Gospel we pray a psalm. Afterward we listen as a homily is preached.

We offer gifts to God. We bring bread and wine to the altar. With them, we offer ourselves and our works to God. The bread and wine are consecrated and become Jesus. He offers himself to God the Father and we offer him too.

God offers us a gift. Jesus comes to us in Holy Communion. We are filled with grace. We are sent from Mass to live and share the Good News.

A Catholic VIP

St. Pius X (1835–1914)

Giuseppe Sarto was a priest from Italy who felt called to work for the poor. Instead he was assigned to teach at the seminary. After becoming a bishop and a cardinal, he was elected pope. He took the motto "Renew all things in Christ." As Pope Pius X, he urged people to receive the Eucharist often. And he made it possible for children as young as seven to receive Communion, something that wasn't done at the time. This holy pope encouraged Scripture study and social action. In vain, he worked to prevent World War I, and died soon after it began. His feast day is August 21.

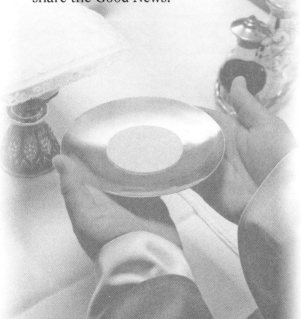

BTW

The word *Mass* comes from the Latin word for "sent." At the end of Mass we are sent to love and serve God.

Did You Know?

We fast for an hour before receiving Communion. We eat or drink only water and medicine and don't chew gum either before or during Mass.

Receiving Communion

Any baptized Catholic who has had proper preparation and is free from serious sin may receive Communion. In the Eucharist, lesser sins are forgiven. How do we receive Communion? We join our minds and hearts with the prayers of preparation said by the priest. We process up with our hands folded. We bow before the sacrament. When the priest or other minister says, "The Body of Christ," we respond, "Amen." We may receive the Host in our hand or on our tongue. To receive in our hand we extend our open hands with the left hand resting on the right one and then step aside and with our right hand place the Host in our mouth. When the Precious Blood is offered, we bow. At the words, "The Blood of Christ," we respond, "Amen." We receive the chalice and take a sip from it. Even though we receive just part of the consecrated bread or wine, we receive Jesus, our God and Savior.

Scripture Link

Multiplication of Loaves

One day more than five thousand people had followed Jesus. He asked Philip where they could buy bread for them. Philip said, "Even six months' pay would not buy enough bread for each of them to get a little." Andrew pointed out that a boy had five loaves and two fish. Jesus had the apostles make the people sit. Then he took the bread, gave thanks, and passed it out. He did the same with the fish. The leftovers filled twelve baskets! The next day, Jesus spoke about eating his flesh and drinking his blood to have eternal life. Many people couldn't accept that and stopped following him. The miracle of bread and fish foreshadows the Eucharist, where Jesus feeds millions.

(cf. Jn 6:1–14, 54, 66)

From My Heart

O sacrament most holy,
O sacrament divine,
all praise and all thanksgiving
be every moment thine.

Now Act!

Write a prayer
to say to Jesus after
receiving him
in Communion.

Recap

• •

- **The Eucharist, our most perfect worship, is the source and high point of Christian life.**

- **Jesus gave us the Eucharist at the Last Supper as a memorial of his death and resurrection.**

- **Through the Eucharist the death and resurrection of Jesus is re-presented; he offers himself to the Father, and we offer ourselves and him.**

- **At Mass through the power of the Holy Spirit and the priest's words, bread and wine become Jesus.**

- **Receiving Jesus in Holy Communion unites us and helps us grow in holiness.**

24

What Is the Sacrament of Penance?

Catechism *In the sacrament of Penance and Reconciliation, God forgives sins committed after Baptism and we are reconciled with him and the Church (cf. no. 1422).*

Recall an occasion when you did something wrong that hurt someone. How did you feel? At times like this we say our **conscience** (KON-shuhns), our sense of right and wrong, bothers us. We feel guilty, sad, and ashamed. Maybe we can't sleep. Three words can free us from these bad feelings: *I forgive you.* Jesus gave us a sacrament in which we hear God say those words to us through a priest: the sacrament of Penance and Reconciliation. It is one of the two sacraments of healing. The other is the sacrament of the Anointing of the Sick.

Jesus Heals

Jesus is called the Divine Physician. He healed people's bodies and souls. As he went about curing diseases and disabilities, Jesus also told people that their sins were forgiven. He could do this because he was God, the one who was offended by sin. Only God can forgive sins. Over and over Jesus taught that God was merciful and eager to have sinners change their hearts and come back to him. On the night of the resurrection, Jesus gave his apostles the power to forgive sins. He breathed on them and said, "Receive the Holy Spirit. If you forgive the sins of any, they are forgiven them" (Jn 20:22–23). Today the apostles' successors, our bishops and priests, forgive us, or give us **absolution**. They do so in the name of Jesus in the sacrament of Penance.

Did You Know?

Jesus told a parable about a sheep that wanders off. The shepherd leaves ninety-nine others to look for it. When he finds the lost sheep, he rejoices. Jesus also told a parable about a woman who loses a coin. She searches the house until she finds it. Then she calls her neighbors to celebrate (cf. Lk 15:1-10). These two parables show how much God cares for each of us.

Reconciliation

Sin is an act or an omission (a failure to act) in which we fail to love. When we disobey God by sin, we separate ourselves from him and from other members of the Church. With grace from the Holy Spirit, we feel sorry for our sin and **repent**. We want to turn our lives around. This change for the better is called **conversion**. Because Jesus atoned, or made up for all sin by his death on the cross, we can be friends with God again. We can be forgiven and reconciled with him through the sacrament of Penance.

BTW

The Hebrew word for sin means "missing the mark." When we sin, we miss the mark of holiness.

Elements of the Sacrament

To be forgiven, three things are required:

1. We must have **contrition.** That is, we must be truly sorry for our sin. We might be sorry because our sin offends God who loves us so much. Or we might be sorry because we don't like the consequences of our sins. Our contrition is only true if we intend not to commit the sin again.

2. We must **confess** the sin to a priest, who represents Jesus. We are only required to confess serious sins, but it is a good idea to confess venial sins too.

3. We must do **penance**, something that will help make up for our sins, show God how sorry we are, and strengthen our spiritual life. This can be prayers or good acts. The priest assigns us a penance.

BTW

Priests are bound not to reveal what a person confesses in the sacrament of Penance. This secrecy is known as the **seal of confession**.

Did You Know?

An **indulgence** (in-DUHL-juhns) is the erasing of all or part of the punishment that is the result of our sins. An indulgence is gained by prayers and good works as described by the Church. It applies to us the store of graces won by Christ and the saints.

Examining Our Conscience

To prepare for the sacrament of Penance, we pray to the Holy Spirit and then think back over our lives since our last confession. Our sins will jump out at us. A sin is only a sin if it is something wrong, if we have time to think before we commit it, and if we really intend to commit it. **Temptations**, which are urges to sin, are not sins. Neither are accidents. To identify our sins, it helps to review the Ten Commandments. See page 227.

The Rite

There is a Rite for people to celebrate the sacrament as a group and then confess and receive absolution individually. There is another Rite for a group to receive absolution together in case of emergency. But the usual way to celebrate Reconciliation is individually, face to face with the priest, or behind a curtain or screen. Here are the steps:

1. Greet the priest and possibly read a Scripture passage.

2. Confess your sins and say how often you committed them. You might tell why you committed them.

3. Listen to the priest who will talk to you a little and give you a penance. Ask any questions you may have.

4. Pray an Act of Contrition.

5. Listen to the words of absolution.

6. Do your penance as soon as possible.

Effects of the Sacrament

The sacrament of Penance forgives sins and removes the punishment they deserve. Also, the grace we receive in the sacrament of Penance makes us stronger against temptations. It brings us peace because it makes us right with God again and with the Church.

Brainstorm

Discuss the different meanings we have for the word "peace." Why is the sacrament of Penance "the sacrament of peace"?

A Catholic VIP

St. John Mary Vianney (1786–1859)

John Vianney grew up on a farm during the French Revolution when people weren't free to practice the faith. He was ordained a priest when religious freedom was restored. John became Curé (pastor) of Ars, a village where people didn't practice their faith. Some people resented John and gave him a hard time. But his prayers and love changed their hearts. Soon people from all over came to him for confession and advice. He heard confessions for ten, sometimes as much as fifteen, hours a day. A railroad line was built to Ars to handle all his visitors. St. John lived a life of service, prayer, fasting, and penance. His feast day is August 4.

Scripture Link

Jesus Pardons a Woman

One day Jesus was eating at the house of a religious leader. Suddenly a woman who was known to be a sinner came into the room. She was crying because she was sorry for her sins, and her tears fell on Jesus's feet. The woman wiped the tears away with her long hair, kissed his feet, and poured precious oil on them. The religious leader didn't think Jesus should let this sinner touch him. But Jesus declared the woman's sins were forgiven because she showed much love. Then he said to the woman, "Your sins are forgiven. Go in peace."

(cf. Lk 7:36–50)

From My Heart

Pray an
Act of Contrition.
See page 233.

Now Act!

Begin the
habit of
examining your
conscience
every night.

Recap

- God forgives our sins in the sacrament of Penance so that we are reconciled to him and to one another as members of the Church.

- Priests give us absolution in the name of Jesus.

- To be forgiven we must be sorry for our sins, confess them to the priest, and do penance.

25

What Does the Anointing of the Sick Do?

Catechism   *The sacrament of the Anointing of the Sick strengthens those who are ill (cf. no. 1511).*

When we have a toothache, a stomachache, a broken bone, a cold, or other illness, nothing interests us. We don't feel like doing anything, and may even become sad or grouchy.

Jesus once said, "I came that they may have life, and have it abundantly" (Jn 10:10). One way he renews our life is by conquering our diseases. By dying and rising, Jesus healed the whole world of the wound of sin. When he walked the roads of Israel, he cured broken bodies, minds, and hearts. Today Jesus continues to bring life through the sacrament of the Anointing of the Sick.

History of the Sacrament

Jesus told his apostles, "Cure the sick, raise the dead, cleanse the lepers, cast out demons" (Mt 10:8). The apostles "anointed with oil many who were sick and cured them" (Mk 6:13). Anointing the sick was common in the early Church. In a letter St. James states, "Are any among you sick? They should call for the elders [priests] of the church and have them pray over them, anointing them with oil in the name of the Lord. The prayer of faith will save the sick . . . and anyone who has committed sins will be forgiven" (Jas 5:14–15). Today the sacrament is still administered by priests and supported by the faith of the community.

BTW

For centuries this sacrament was given only to those who were dying and was called Extreme Unction.

A Note on Illness

Illness makes us face our limitations and reminds us of death. The experience of being ill can turn a person against God or inspire a person to seek God. Because Christ suffered, suffering now has meaning. The sick can unite themselves to Christ's passion and death and offer their suffering for the good of God's people and as penance for their sins. By doing this, they participate in Christ's saving work and add to the Church's holiness.

Brainstorm

We all know of people who are sick or who have been sick. They may be in the hospital, in a nursing home, or at home with us. What can you do to show love for those who are sick?

A Catholic VIP

St. John of God (1495–1550)

St. John was a shepherd who became a soldier and then the owner of a Catholic bookstore. One day while listening to a sermon by St. John of Avila, John had a spiritual experience. Because he seemed to suffer a breakdown, John was put in a hospital. There he understood God's call to care for the sick and poor. John worked for the needy people in Granada, Spain. Other men joined him and together they formed a religious community called the Order of Hospitallers. St. John died as a result of trying to save a young man from drowning. Today Brothers Hospitallers work all over the world. St. John's feast day is March 8.

Effects of the Sacrament

The Anointing of the Sick has many benefits:

- It helps the sick to be witnesses of Christian hope. They receive grace to bear suffering, fight illness, and resist temptation.

- The sacrament brings peace of heart, and trust in God replaces anxiety and fear.

- The sick receive grace to unite themselves to Jesus's suffering and death.

- The sacrament also forgives sin if the sick person has not been able to receive the sacrament of Penance immediately before the anointing.

- If this is the last anointing, it gives strength for the final journey.

- The Anointing of the Sick may restore health if this is for the spiritual good of the sick person.

Did You Know?

Oil of the Sick is blessed by the bishop at the Chrism Mass on Holy Thursday.

BTW

It is very meaningful when the Anointing of the Sick takes place within the celebration of the Eucharist. This shows how the community supports the sick person.

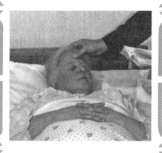

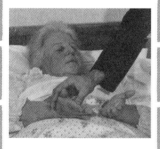

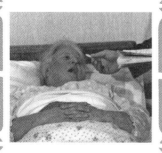

Who May Receive the Sacrament?

Anyone in danger of death may receive the Anointing of the Sick. This includes the dangerously ill, the elderly, and those facing surgery. It is not for minor illnesses like a cold. A person may receive the sacrament of the Anointing of the Sick more than once. We should encourage the sick to take advantage of this gift.

How the Sacrament Is Celebrated

The Anointing of the Sick may take place in church, in a hospital, or in a home. It may be for one person or a group. The sacrament begins with an act of repentance followed by a reading from Scripture. Then the priest lays hands on the heads of the sick people and prays over them in the faith of the Church. He anoints them by making the Sign of the Cross with oil on the forehead and each hand. Anointing the forehead, he prays, "Through this holy anointing may the Lord in his love and mercy help you with the grace of the Holy Spirit." As he anoints their hands, he prays, "May the Lord who frees you from sin save you and raise you up."

Viaticum

Those who are close to death also receive the Eucharist. This reminds them that Jesus promised eternal life to all who eat his flesh and drink his blood. This final Communion is called **Viaticum** (vy-AT-i-kuhm), a Latin word which means "with you on the way."

Care of the Sick

Jesus had compassion for the sick. We, his followers, can show the same loving concern for them. In a parable, Jesus identified himself with the sick. He said that people entered the kingdom because when he was sick, they visited him (cf. Mt 25:39).

From My Heart

Think of people you know who are sick. Pray to Jesus for them.

Scripture Link

Jesus Gives Life to a Woman and a Girl

A man named Jairus once begged Jesus to come to his house. His twelve-year-old daughter was dying. As Jesus went, a crowd was pressing on him. One woman had been sick for twelve years and had spent all her money on doctors. She came up behind Jesus and touched the fringe of his clothes. At once she was well again. Jesus said, "Someone touched me. I felt power go out." The woman came forth and declared her healing. Jesus said her faith had cured her. At that, the servants of Jairus came with the news that his daughter had died. Still Jesus went to the house. He entered it with only Peter, John, James, and the girl's parents. To the weeping mourners Jesus said, "She is not dead but sleeping." Then he took the girl by the hand and said, "Child, get up!" She got up, and Jesus told her amazed parents to give her something to eat.

(cf. Lk 8:40–56)

Attend a communal celebration of the Anointing of the Sick, or ask someone who's been anointed what it was like.

Recap

- The Anointing of the Sick gives sick and elderly people the grace to bear suffering, fight illness, and resist temptation.

- This sacrament brings peace and the grace to unite one's suffering with the suffering of Jesus.

- The Rite of the sacrament includes the laying on of hands and anointing with oil.

- Viaticum is the last Communion of the dying.

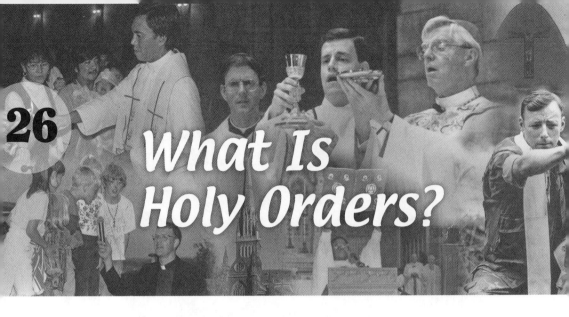

26

What Is Holy Orders?

Catechism *Through Holy Orders the mission Jesus gave his apostles is carried out in the Church until the end of time (cf. no. 1536).*

✠ In 1921, Father Edward Flanagan founded Boys Town in Nebraska. Today it helps children and families all over the United States.

✠ Archbishop Oscar Romero spoke out for the poor and for victims of El Salvador's civil war. Because of this, he was assassinated during Mass in 1980.

✠ Day after day priests in your community celebrate the sacraments and help your community live by the values of Jesus.

These men have been called to a special role. They have received Holy Orders, one of the two sacraments that consecrate people for service to the whole Church. The other sacrament is Matrimony. Both sacraments build up the People of God. In this chapter we will look at Holy Orders, the sacrament that consecrates bishops, priests, and deacons. Through these men, called the **clergy**, Jesus guides his Church.

Priesthood

In Old Testament times, priests were those who offered sacrifices and prayed for the people. Jesus is the high priest who offered a unique sacrifice on the cross once and for all. Today he makes this sacrifice present in the Eucharist through his priests. Through Baptism, all of us share in the priesthood of Christ. We follow his example and offer our lives to God. But the priesthood of priests and bishops is different. The sacrament of Holy Orders makes them representatives of Christ. Through these ordained ministers, Jesus is present to us and acts for us. They also act in our name when presenting our prayer, especially when offering the Eucharistic sacrifice.

Ordination

There are three degrees of holy orders: the **episcopate** (i-PIS-co-pate) or bishops, **presbyterate** (prez-BI-ter-ate) or priests, and **diaconate** (dee-AK-uhn-ate) or deacons. Only bishops can administer the sacrament of Holy Orders. Men are ordained by the laying on of hands and the words of consecration. Usually priests are not married, since they are called to give their whole life and all their energy to God by serving his people. In the Eastern Churches, however, priests are sometimes married and have families. Married men can become deacons, but after ordination, deacons may not marry. Like Baptism and Confirmation, the sacrament of Holy Orders imparts a permanent spiritual character.

A Catholic VIP

St. Damien of Molokai (1840–1889)

St. Damien was born in Belgium. He joined a missionary order called the Congregation of the Sacred Hearts of Jesus and Mary, and was ordained a priest in Hawaii. He volunteered to work with people who suffered from leprosy (now known as Hansen's disease). They were isolated on the island of Molokai. Left alone in their suffering, the people lived there without medical care or spiritual help. When Fr. Damien arrived, he helped the community build a church and grow crops. Fr. Damien nursed the sick and with great love and respect buried those who died. He saw that laws were kept and that houses, schools, a hospital, and an orphanage were built. After being a true father to the people of Molokai for sixteen years, St. Damien contracted leprosy and died. His feast day is May 10.

Bishops

Bishops have the fullness of ordination. They are successors to the apostles, who received an outpouring of the Holy Spirit from Christ after the resurrection. Through their consecration, bishops are empowered to teach the faith and govern and sanctify the Church. As the vicar, or agent, of Christ, each bishop oversees a particular **diocese** (DY-uh-sees), or group of parishes. But he belongs to the college of bishops, which cares for the whole Church. The pope, the bishop of Rome, is the visible bond of Church unity. He is the universal pastor. A bishop's church is called a **cathedral** (kuh-THEE-druhl). As signs of his authority, a bishop wears a tall hat called a **miter** (MY-ter) and carries a staff called a **crosier** (KROH-zher).

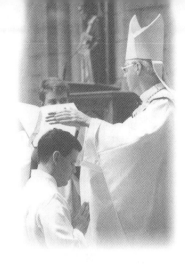

BTW

Like everyone, priests can be weak and even sin. However, their flaws do not affect the grace we receive from the sacraments they celebrate.

Brainstorm

What virtues do priests, deacons, and bishops especially need? How can you or your family show support for your clergy?

Priests

Priests work with their bishops in carrying out the mission of Christ. Acting in the person of Jesus, priests preach the Gospel, shepherd the faithful, and celebrate divine worship. When celebrating Mass and the sacraments, a priest wears a **stole**, a strip of material, around his shoulders, as the symbol of ordination. Priests are assigned to parishes or other offices by their bishops. They usually live in a **rectory** (REK-tuh-ree). Besides diocesan priests, there are priests who belong to religious communities and take religious vows. Priests are privileged to share God's loving care with people in their times of joy and struggle.

Deacons

You may have at least one deacon at your parish. At Mass he is at the altar wearing a stole draped over his left shoulder. The word *deacon* comes from a word that means "service." Like Christ, a deacon is a servant of all. He may perform Baptisms, assist at the Eucharist, witness marriages, proclaim the Gospel and preach, preside over funerals, and do charitable works. Like the other clergy members, deacons perform apostolic ministry.

Did You Know?

There are two kinds of deacons: permanent deacons and deacons who are on the way to priesthood called transitional deacons.

Scripture Link

Jesus and Peter

After the resurrection, Jesus made breakfast on the shore for Peter and other apostles. Then he asked Peter if he loved him more than the others. Peter replied yes. Jesus then said, "Feed my lambs." Again Jesus asked Peter if he loved him and Peter replied yes. Jesus said, "Feed my sheep." A third time Jesus asked Peter, "Do you love me?" Again Peter said yes. And Jesus said, "Feed my sheep." Then Jesus foretold Peter's martyrdom and said, "Follow me." Peter the fisherman became the shepherd of Christ's flock.

(cf. Jn 21:15–19)

From My Heart

Ask the Holy Spirit to call many more good men to serve the Church as priests and deacons. Reflect on the vocation to which God might be calling you.

Now Act!

Find out what is involved in becoming a priest. Think of a way you could help someone who expresses the desire for priesthood.

Recap

- Through the laying on of hands and words of consecration in Holy Orders men are set apart to serve and guide the Church.

- Bishops, successors of the apostles who have the fullness of ordination, teach, govern, and sanctify the Church.

- Priests represent Christ and offer the Eucharist on our behalf.

- Deacons assist at liturgies and do charitable works.

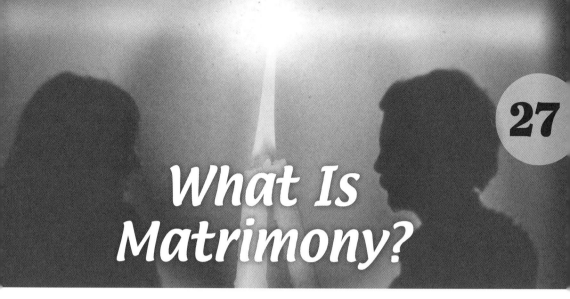

What Is Matrimony?

27

Catechism *Matrimony is the sacrament that gives a couple the grace to love each other as Christ loves the Church and helps them to be one and to be holy (cf. no. 1661).*

Weddings are joyful celebrations. At the time of Jesus, Jewish weddings could last a week! Throughout history and in all cultures, people have married. A couple is bound together by a legal contract, but Jesus raised marriage to new dignity. He made it the sacrament we call Matrimony. Along with Holy Orders, Matrimony is considered a sacrament of service. Together, a married man and woman help each other to be holy, to welcome and raise children, and to build up the Church and society. In Matrimony Jesus gives baptized persons the graces they need to carry out this challenging mission.

Marriage: God's Idea

When God created Adam and Eve, he intended man and woman to love each other. Their lives were to be united "so they are no longer two but one" (Mt 19:6). This unity can be compared to the flames of two candles joined to make one new flame. The love of a married couple is intended to be an image of the love among the three Persons of the Trinity that makes them One. It is also an image of the love between Christ and the Church. Moreover, by giving birth to children, couples are co-creators with God. God told Adam and Eve, our first parents, "Be fruitful and multiply, and fill the earth" (Gen 1:28).

Did You Know?

St. Paul calls the Church the Bride of Christ. Jesus loves the Church and gave his life for her. He spoke of heaven as a wedding feast where we will be united with him forever.

Brainstorm

What qualities in a good friendship will also help in marriage? What have you learned about love and Christian life from your family?

BTW

Wedding rings are a sign of everlasting love.

A Covenant

Marriage is a covenant, a solemn agreement, in which a man and a woman vow before God and witnesses to love each other and no one else with a special love that will give life and last until death. This love mirrors the unending love that Jesus has for his Church. For this reason, most Catholic marriages take place during the celebration of the Eucharist, when Christ shows his love for us and unites himself to us.

The bride and groom give the sacrament to each other by pronouncing vows. They give a gift of themselves to one another. A priest or deacon receives their vows in the name of the Church and gives them the Church's blessing.

Did You Know?

God calls some people to be single and to use their gifts for the good of the Church. Whether you are single or married, your gifts can be used by God and shared with others.

St. Elizabeth of Hungary (1207–1231)

Strength in Difficulty

Loving someone faithfully for a lifetime can be very difficult. That is why the sacrament of Matrimony provides grace to strengthen couples. A Christian marriage is like a triangle. It involves not only a man and a woman, but also God. Because original sin has left us weak and sinful, sometimes a couple can no longer live together. They may be separated for a time.

Although the couple may file for a legal divorce, this does not end their marriage. The Church continues to believe the teaching of Jesus: "What God has joined together, let no one separate" (Mt 19:6).

Persons whose marriage partners are still alive may not marry someone else. Sometimes the Church grants an **annulment** (uh-NUHL-munt) if there is proof that the marriage was not a true marriage. Only after an annulment may the man and woman marry again.

St. Elizabeth of Hungary was the daughter of the king of Hungary. At the age of fourteen she married Ludwig, a good nobleman of Germany. They had three children. Ludwig once declared that he wouldn't trade a gold mountain for Elizabeth. When he died on the way to a Crusade, a war fought for the Church, Elizabeth cried out, "It is as though the world is dead to me." Elizabeth dressed simply and was very generous to the poor. Angered by this, her in-laws threw her out of the castle. But her friends brought her back, and Elizabeth built a hospital where she worked for the poor. A legend holds that once when she carried bread for the poor in her cloak, Ludwig opened it to see what she was carrying and found roses. St. Elizabeth's feast day is November 17.

Families

Children are the special gift of marriage. They are a living sign of their parents' love and union. Children often have characteristics of both parents. For example, you might have your father's nose and your mother's sense of humor. Children enrich the lives of their parents and add to the family of God. All married couples are called to be open to raising children. Those who are unable to have children of their own are encouraged to adopt or foster children.

Parents are the first teachers of their children. In particular, they are meant to teach their children how to live the Christian life, how to love. Catholic families are sometimes called "the domestic Church," which is like calling them "the Church at home." Members pray together, celebrate the sacraments, and practice Christian virtues, above all, love. Families are the building blocks of society and the Church. When family life is good, the whole world is enriched.

> **BTW**
>
> Jesus chose to grow up in a family. He, Mary, and Joseph are called the Holy Family.

Scripture Link

Wedding at Cana

Jesus worked his first miracle at a wedding in Cana where he, his mother, and the apostles were guests. Noticing that the wine had run out, Mary mentioned it to Jesus. He asked, "Woman, what is that to you and me?" Still, Mary told the servants to do whatever he said. Jesus had the servants fill six large jars with water and then take some to the headwaiter. When this man tasted it, the water had turned into wine. He said to the bridegroom, "Everyone serves the good wine first, but you have kept the best wine until now." The presence of Jesus at this wedding and his miracle show the goodness of marriage and God's care for married persons.

(cf. Jn 2:1–11)

From My Heart

Take some time to pray for all the married couples you know. Ask the Holy Spirit to bless them with the virtues they need to live marriage in a holy way.

Now Act!

Write a paragraph explaining how a movie or TV show does or does not present a good marriage or a good family.

Recap

• The sacrament of Matrimony provides a married couple with the graces they need to stay united, to become holy, and to raise children.

• A man and woman confer the sacrament on each other by pronouncing marriage vows.

• Married couples love each other and no one else with a special love that lasts until death.

• Families are the domestic church in which children learn to live as Christians.

28

How Can We Make Good Choices?

Catechism *All Christians are called to holiness. In Matthew 5:48, Jesus said, "Be perfect, as your heavenly Father is perfect" (cf. no. 2013).*

You probably know the story of Pinocchio, a wooden puppet carved by Geppetto. The puppet can become a real boy if he is brave, honest, unselfish, and follows his conscience. A cricket serves as Pinocchio's conscience and gives him good advice. After getting into all kinds of trouble, Pinocchio acts unselfishly and does become human.

Two Ways

Acts that can be labeled right or wrong are called **moral acts**. Like Pinocchio, we are constantly faced with decisions to do right or wrong. We too have a conscience, but it is an inner voice, not a cricket!

Conscience is the power of our minds to judge what is right or wrong. We are free to choose which way to go: the path of good or the path of evil. Jesus is our example for making right choices. By following his way of love and obeying his commandments, we fulfill our vocation, the call to be holy. This insures that we will become the people God planned us to be when he created us. We will share divine life as God's adopted sons and daughters.

Did You Know?

A **vice** is a bad habit.
The **capital sins** are vices that are the source of all sins:

Pride is belief that I am better than others.
Avarice is being greedy and wanting more than my share.
Envy is feeling jealous of someone else.
Wrath is unjust anger.
Lust is an unrestrained desire for pleasure, especially sexual pleasure.
Gluttony is eating and drinking in excess.
Sloth is giving in to laziness.

New Life in Christ

Adam and Eve made a very bad choice. By disobeying God, they not only broke off their relationship with him, but also that of the whole human race. But God showed mercy. Jesus, by his death and rising, saved everyone from sin and brought us divine life. Being cleansed from sin and sharing in God's holiness is called **justification**. It is the work of the Holy Spirit. At Baptism, we receive the new life won by Christ. We are then called to make choices throughout our lives that reflect the love of God alive in us. Our consciences guide us, but because of original sin, we sometimes have to struggle hard against temptation. If we fail and sin, our loving and merciful God is ready to forgive us again.

Morality

Whether an act is good or bad depends on three things:

1. *The deed itself*. This might be evil, like lying, or good, like helping the poor.

2. *A person's intention*. Doing a good act for a bad motive spoils the act. On the other hand, though, a good intention never makes a bad deed good. If I steal a bike in order to give it to my brother, the act is still wrong.

3. *The circumstances and consequences*. These can make an act more or less good or evil. They can also make a person more or less responsible. For instance, if you forget to set your alarm clock and you miss the school bus, you are late for class, but you are less responsible than if you had missed the bus on purpose.

We are to act according to our conscience. However, we need to have an *informed* conscience. This means we must make an effort to learn what is right and wrong from Jesus, his Church, and Scripture. Otherwise, we will be responsible for acting in ignorance.

Did You Know?

Some ways to fight temptation and grow in virtue are praying, receiving Holy Communion, going to confession, having good friends, and learning about the saints.

Brainstorm

What are some things that might lead you into temptation? How can you best avoid them? In what ways did Jesus show us how to live holy lives?

BTW

God gives us special, on-the-spot help to do good called **actual grace**.

Sins

Sin is a failure to love God and others. **Mortal sin** is a "deadly" sin that separates a person from God. This sin has three conditions: (1) The act must be serious, (2) the person must know how serious it is, and (3) the person must deliberately decide to do it. Any other sin is **venial sin**, a less serious sin which weakens our friendship with God. Repeated sins can smother a person's conscience. Likewise, our personal sins can result in **social sins**, which are sins that everyone at a certain time overlooks, such as slavery, injustice, and waste of natural resources.

From My Heart

Tonight think about chances you had to show love in the past week. How did you respond? Ask Jesus to help you to be more loving tomorrow.

Scripture Link

Virtuous People

Happy are those
who do not follow the advice of the wicked,
or take the path that sinners tread . . .
They are like trees
planted by streams of water,
which yield their fruit in its season,
and their leaves do not wither.
In all that they do, they prosper.   (Ps 1:1, 3)

Virtues

A **virtue** is a habit or attitude of doing good that is formed by God's grace and by our effort. Practicing virtues leads to holiness and to God. All virtues are related to these four **cardinal moral virtues**:

Prudence is recognizing what is good and knowing how to achieve it.

Justice is giving God and neighbor what is due to them.

Fortitude is the courage to stand firm and fearless in face of trials in doing good.

Temperance is living with moderation in regard to pleasures and the world's goods.

The three **theological virtues** are gifts of God that relate directly to him and make us act more like him:

Faith is believing God and all he has revealed and what the Church teaches.

Hope is trusting in Christ's promises and the grace of the Holy Spirit that our desire for eternal life in heaven will be fulfilled.

Charity is loving God above all things and our neighbor as ourselves for the love of God.

A Catholic VIP

St. Dominic Savio (1842–1857)

Although Dominic lived only fourteen years, his life of heroic virtue led to his canonization. Born in Italy, Dominic learned the Christian life from his parents. On the day of his First Communion, he wrote four promises. The last one was not to sin, no matter what the cost. At school, with St. Don Bosco as his spiritual guide, Dominic learned to be holy in ordinary ways. He prayed much, did his duties well, didn't complain, and encouraged other boys to avoid sin. Dominic's dream was to be a priest, but illness took his life. He died after exclaiming, "Oh, what wonderful things I see." St. Dominic's feast day is May 6.

In a newspaper find examples of sins as well as virtues and their effects. Reflect on these and write a paragraph explaining why it is better to practice virtue than to commit sin.

Now Act!

Recap

- **Being right with God and sharing in his holiness is called justification.**

- **We are free to choose right or wrong with the help of conscience, which is our mind deciding whether an act is good or evil.**

- **The goodness or badness of an act depends on the act, the intention, the circumstances, and the consequences.**

- **Sin is a failure to love God and others.**

- **A vice is a bad habit, and a virtue is a good habit.**

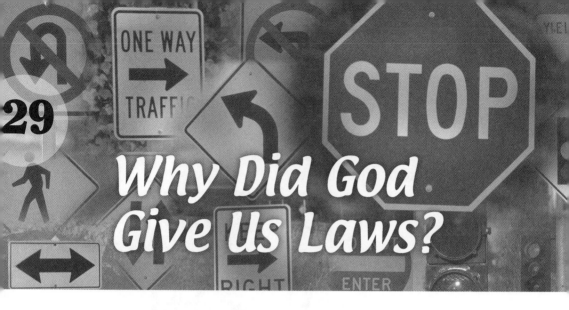

Why Did God Give Us Laws?

Catechism *God's laws let us know the acts that lead to eternal happiness and those acts that turn us away from him and his love (cf. no. 1950).*

Imagine if there were no traffic laws. People wouldn't have to stop at stop signs or red lights. They could go any speed on any road. They wouldn't have to wear seat belts. The roads would not be a very safe place! Good laws are a blessing. They promote life for all of us and help us enjoy good relationships with others. A **law** is a rule of conduct made by a lawful authority for the common good. A good law never goes against the law of God. Just as cities and nations have laws, God has given us laws to guide us, protect us, and lead us to eternal happiness.

Natural Law

All of us have **natural law** written in our hearts. This is how we are able to tell the difference between good and evil. For example, even if your parents hadn't taught you it was wrong to steal, you would still have a sense that stealing is wrong. Natural law is the same for every person, of every time and place, and it never changes. It binds the human family together and is the foundation for our moral choices.

The Revealed Law

Many truths contained in natural law were revealed by God in the Law he gave to the Israelites. During the Exodus, on Mount Sinai, God gave Moses stone tablets on which were written ten laws. These laws made it clear how to live as his people. These Ten Commandments are also called the **Decalogue** (DEK-uh-log), which means "ten words." Then God and the people of Israel made a covenant that Israel would be God's people, and that he would be their only God. The people declared, "We will do everything that the Lord has told us" (cf. Ex 24:3). The commandments are not just for the Israelites, but for us too. When a man asked Jesus how to inherit eternal life, Jesus told him to keep the commandments. These laws tell us how to love. The first three explain how to love God, and the other seven are about loving others.

The Commandments

1. I am the Lord, your God. You shall not have other gods besides me.
2. You shall not take the name of the Lord your God in vain.
3. Remember to keep holy the Lord's day.
4. Honor your father and your mother.
5. You shall not kill.
6. You shall not commit adultery.
7. You shall not steal.
8. You shall not bear false witness against your neighbor.
9. You shall not covet your neighbor's wife.
10. You shall not covet your neighbor's goods.

The Sermon on the Mount

The teachings of Jesus perfect the commandments. In the Sermon on the Mount he explained that we are to go beyond the commandments. For example, Jesus said, "Love your enemies and pray for those who persecute you" (Mt 5:44). Jesus also gave us the eight **Beatitudes**, which state attitudes we need to reach the promised kingdom. Each beatitude begins with "Blessed" which means "happy." Living according to the Beatitudes leads to happiness. In other words, Jesus showed us how to be like our heavenly Father. He summed up his teaching in the Golden Rule: "Do to others as you would have them do to you" (Mt 7:12).

Brainstorm

For each commandment, what word or two sums up the positive thing it tells us to do? For example, the fourth commandment means "obey." These keywords will help you remember the Ten Commandments. How are the Beatitudes a description of Jesus?

The Beatitudes

Blessed are the poor in spirit, for theirs is the kingdom of heaven.

Blessed are those who mourn, for they will be comforted.

Blessed are the meek, for they will inherit the earth.

Blessed are those who hunger and thirst for righteousness, for they will be filled.

Blessed are the merciful, for they will receive mercy.

Blessed are the pure in heart, for they will see God.

Blessed are the peacemakers, for they will be called children of God.

Blessed are those who are persecuted for righteousness' sake, for theirs is the kingdom of heaven (Mt 5:1–10).

A New Commandment

At the Last Supper, Jesus gave us a new commandment. He said, "Just as I have loved you, you also should love one another" (Jn 13:34). This is a high standard, considering that Jesus died for love of us!

A Catholic VIP

St. Thomas More (1478–1535)

St. Thomas More gave up his life rather than break God's laws. This father of four was a lawyer and a friend to King Henry VIII of England. He became chancellor of England, second only to the king. When Henry wanted to divorce his wife to marry Anne Boleyn, the pope refused to approve this and so did Thomas. Then Henry made people sign a document declaring him head of the Church in England. Thomas would not sign it, so for over a year he was imprisoned in the Tower of London. Because he stood fast against pressure to give in, Thomas was beheaded. He said, "I die the king's good servant, but God's first." We celebrate St. Thomas More's feast day on June 22.

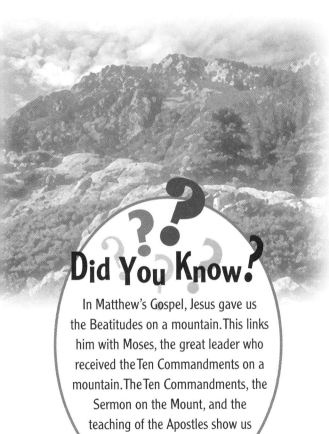

Did You Know?

In Matthew's Gospel, Jesus gave us the Beatitudes on a mountain. This links him with Moses, the great leader who received the Ten Commandments on a mountain. The Ten Commandments, the Sermon on the Mount, and the teaching of the Apostles show us the way to the Kingdom of God.

Scripture Link

The Greatest Commandment

Once a lawyer asked Jesus what the greatest commandment was. Jesus replied, "You shall love the Lord your God with all your heart, and with all your soul, and with all your mind." He then said that a second one is like it and stated, "You shall love your neighbor as yourself." That greatest commandment is part of the Shema, an important prayer from Scripture that Jewish people pray. Loving God is what we were created to do. It is the only way to happiness.

(cf. Mt 22:34–39)

Did You Know?

The five **precepts** (rules) **of the Church** help us grow in holiness. You can find them on page 228.

Write a letter to God, thanking him for his friendship and love for us, and asking for help with something that may be difficult.

From My Heart

Now Act!

Memorize the
Ten Commandments
and the Beatitudes
because they are
important.

Recap

- God's laws guide us, protect us, and lead us to eternal happiness.

- The Ten Commandments God gave to Moses show us how to love God and others.

- Jesus gave us the Beatitudes, which describe attitudes that lead to the kingdom of God.

- The new commandment of Jesus is to love others as he loved us.

How Do We Love God Above All?

30

Catechism *We obey the First Commandment by adoring God, praying to him, and keeping vows made to him (cf. no. 2135).*

A popular Christian song calls God "awesome." The God we Christians believe in is not only awesome, but he is the only God. People in many cultures around the world and throughout history have worshiped and sacrificed to many gods and goddesses. God's revelation to Abraham taught us that there is only one God, a concept shared by Jews, Christians, and Muslims. Abraham's people had a personal relationship with this one God, who loves us.

The First Commandment protects this relationship and nurtures our love for God. It forbids the worship of other "gods" which really are not gods at all. We call these false gods **idols**.

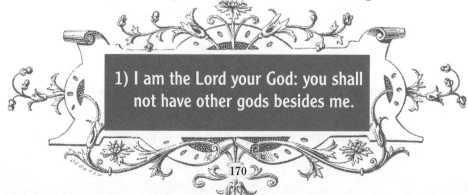

1) I am the Lord your God: you shall not have other gods besides me.

BTW

Belief in one God is **monotheism** (mon-o-THEE-iz-uhm). Belief in many gods is **polytheism** (pol-ee-THEE-iz-uhm).

Worship: Our Response

God is worthy of our praise and thanks because he is God and because he is our creator. We keep the First Commandment by honoring God and keeping his commandments. One way to honor God is by spending time with him in prayer. We do this when we have a habit of praying morning, night, and meal prayers. We worship God as individuals and together with a community in church and in our family. Praying to God deepens our relationship with him.

We also worship God by making sacrifices to him. A **sacrifice** is a gift given to God. At Mass we offer our hearts and all we do to God in union with the sacrifice of Jesus on the cross. A sacrifice can also be doing something difficult or giving something up. During Lent we make sacrifices to honor God. When we give up ice cream or chocolate for instance, we are giving up something we love in order to show God that we love him even more. This practice makes us more like Jesus, who gave up his life out of love for us.

The virtue of **religion** helps us worship God and live with the theological virtues of faith, hope, and charity.

Brainstorm

Why is it wrong to consider anything more important than God? How can this lead to unhappiness?

Some Challenges to Faith

Atheists, who deny that God exists, sin against faith. People sin against hope when they choose to **despair**, or believe that they are beyond God's help and mercy. People also sin against hope by **presumption**, which means they either think that they can save themselves without God's help or assume that God will save them no matter what they do. Another sin against the First Commandment is **sacrilege**. This is dishonoring persons, things, or places that are holy because they are consecrated to God. For example, it is sacrilege to receive Holy Communion if a serious sin like murder has been committed and the sinner has not gone to the sacrament of Reconciliation.

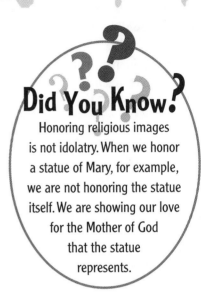

Did You Know?

Honoring religious images is not idolatry. When we honor a statue of Mary, for example, we are not honoring the statue itself. We are showing our love for the Mother of God that the statue represents.

Idolatry

Idolatry (eye-DOL-uh-tree) is the worship of idols. Some of these false gods are objects made of materials such as stone or wood. While Moses was on Mount Sinai, the Israelites made a golden calf and worshiped it. When Moses came down, he was so angry that he threw the tablets of the law on the ground and destroyed the calf.

You might think that you are not in danger of worshiping a statue. However, there are other forms of idols. God needs to be first in our lives. Whenever we put someone or something else before God, it is as if we are worshiping an idol. This idol might be fame, power, money, or pleasure. For example, a person might be so set on making money that he or she ignores God's laws.

Divination

Powers of goodness come from God, but there are also powers of darkness and sin. Sometimes people want information or answers about the future. **Divination** (div-uh-NAY-shuhn) is seeking answers from someone—or something—other than God. This is wrong because it assumes that a creature has God's power. It is also very dangerous. Some forms of divination are the belief that the stars rule our personalities and lives (horoscopes), palm reading, Ouija boards, séances, and fortune telling. Superstitions are wrong too because they replace our trust in God.

A Catholic VIP

St. Isaac Jogues (1607–1646)

Isaac Jogues was a Jesuit priest from France who volunteered to teach Huron Indians of North America about the one God. He was a missionary to the Hurons until he was captured by the Iroquois. For over a year he was enslaved and treated harshly. Then he escaped to France. After recuperating, Father Jogues returned to work among the Iroquois in what is now New York State. When a disease broke out, some Indians thought it was the missionary's fault. One day as Father Jogues entered a longhouse for a peace banquet, an Indian killed him with a tomahawk. The feast day of St. Isaac Jogues and other early North American martyrs is October 19 in the United States and September 26 in Canada. He is a patron saint of Canada.

Vows

A **vow** is a sacred promise made to God in which a Christian pledges to live a certain way or perform a certain act that is pleasing to God. We make baptismal vows. Some people make marriage vows. Others, such as men and women religious, make vows to follow Jesus more closely by living the evangelical counsels of poverty, chastity, and obedience. A fulfilled vow shows the love of God required by the First Commandment.

Scripture Link

Isaiah's Vision

The prophet Isaiah had a vision of God. He saw the Lord sitting on a high throne. The bottom of his robe filled the temple. Six-winged seraphs (angelic creatures) were above him. They called, "Holy, holy, holy is the LORD of hosts; the whole earth is full of his glory." The building shook and filled with smoke. Isaiah said, "Woe is me! I am lost, for I am a man of unclean lips and have seen God." Then, using tongs, one of the angels brought a hot coal from the altar. He touched Isaiah's mouth with it, cleaning him from sin. Then Isaiah heard God say, "Whom shall I send, and who will go for us?" And Isaiah replied, "Here am I; send me!"

(cf. Is 6:1–8)

Did You Know?

When God came to Moses in a burning bush, he told Moses to remove his sandals because the ground he was standing on was holy. We show our belief that God is in church by the way we act there.

From My Heart

Sing or listen to a song praising God.

Or write your own song of praise!

Now Act!

If you could design a billboard to encourage people to keep the First Commandment, what would it say?

Recap

• •

- The First Commandment tells us to worship the one true God rather than idols.

- We honor God by prayer, worship, and sacrifices.

- Sins against the First Commandment are atheism, despair, presumption, sacrilege, and divination.

- Keeping vows is a way of following the First Commandment.

31 Why Do We Treat God's Name With Respect?

Catechism *Respecting God's name shows well-deserved respect for God himself (cf. no. 2144).*

Muslims have ninety-nine beautiful names for Allah, their name for God. These reflect God's qualities and what he does, for example, Most Merciful.

God revealed his personal name to Moses at the burning bush. Out of reverence for this name, the Jewish people do not pronounce it. They substitute a word that means "Lord." We often use the word *God* as if it was God's name. The Second Commandment tells us to treat God's name with respect, because it stands for our most holy God, just as your name stands for you.

> 2) You shall not take the name of the Lord your God in vain.

God's Holy Name

The name of someone we love is special. We like to say it. We also like to hear others call us by name. It's been said that a person's name is to that person the sweetest sound. If our names are so important, how much more important is the name of almighty God!

We use God's name with love and reverence in prayer. For example, in the Our Father we pray, "Hallowed [or holy] be thy name." We begin prayers and other activities "in the name of the Father, and of the Son, and of the Holy Spirit." We should always be careful how we use God's name. The Second Commandment forbids abusing God's name and the name of Jesus Christ. Respecting God's name, and the name of the Virgin Mary and other saints, shows respect for God.

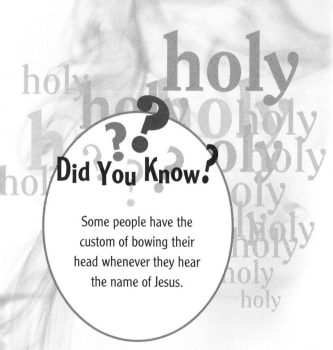

Did You Know?

Some people have the custom of bowing their head whenever they hear the name of Jesus.

A Catholic VIP

St. Bernardine of Siena (1380–1444)

Born in Italy, St. Bernardine was raised by an aunt. After working in a hospital and surviving the plague, Bernardine joined the Franciscans and became a priest. He was famous for preaching throughout Italy and three times refused to be made a bishop. Bernardine had great devotion to the name of Jesus and devised the symbol IHS from the Greek letters that spell Jesus. Once a card maker complained to Bernardine that he was losing business because of the priest's preaching against gambling. Bernardine persuaded the man to make cards with IHS on them instead of playing cards. This made the man wealthy! The Church celebrates the feast of St. Bernardine on May 20.

Disrespecting the Name

Sometimes people say God's name or the name of Jesus to express surprise, pleasure, or anger. This misuse of the holy name is called **profanity** (pro-FAN-i-tee). It is "in vain" because it is calling on God for no purpose. Wouldn't you be frustrated if someone kept calling your name for no reason? Likewise, **cursing**, which is asking God to send evil on someone or something, is in vain. For example, to call on God to send a chair to hell has no effect. It merely insults our good God. Cursing a person is sinful because of the hatred behind it. The careless use of God's name or the name of Jesus is also wrong. Sadly, it's heard often in conversations and in movies and easily becomes a habit.

BTW

People sometimes use the word "swearing" to mean "cursing."

Did You Know?

The *Divine Praises* prayer is intended to make up for profanity and blasphemy.

Brainstorm

How could you respond if you hear someone take God's name in vain?

What expressions can be used instead of God's name to show anger or surprise?

Blasphemy (BLAS-fuh-mee) is another sin against the Second Commandment. This is uttering words of hatred or extreme disrespect against God, Jesus Christ, the Church, the saints, and sacred things.

Taking an **oath**, or **swearing**, is asking God to be a witness that what we say is true. We must reject false oaths, or swearing to something that is not true. That is why St. Thomas More and St. John Fisher refused to take an oath approving of the King of England's unlawful marriage to Anne Boleyn. Also, taking an oath to tell the truth and then not doing so is called **perjury** (PUR-juh-ree). We may take oaths for serious and right reasons. In court, for instance, people are asked to swear to tell the truth. In this case, taking an oath is fine, but then the truth must be told.

Our Names

At Baptism a Christian is to receive a name not contrary to our faith. This is often the name of a saint, who then becomes the person's patron. Or the name may be related to a Christian mystery or virtue. We are to respect all names because they represent people. Scripture tells us that God knows each one of us by name and has our names engraved on the palm of his hand.

From My Heart

Pray the *Divine Praises*
on page 236.

Scripture Link

Vision of Heaven

St. John wrote the last book of the Bible. It is a record of visions he had and was meant to encourage Christians who were being persecuted. In one vision Christ says that he will give to the saints who conquer a white stone on which a new name is written. In another vision, John saw a Lamb, who was Jesus, standing on Mount Zion. With him were 144,000 saints. They had the name of the Lamb and his Father's name written on their foreheads.

(cf. Rev 2:17; 14:1)

Find out the meaning of your name. Learn about your patron saint. If you don't have a saint's name, choose a saint to be your patron.

Now Act!

Recap

• The Second Commandment tells us to respect God's name as well as the name of Jesus Christ.

• Profanity, cursing, blasphemy, and perjury are sins against the Second Commandment.

• At Baptism a Christian receives the name of a saint or a Christian mystery or virtue.

How Do We Keep the Lord's Day Holy?

32

Catechism *The Lord's Day is a day for worship, joy, works of mercy, and relaxing, not for work that would hinder those purposes (cf. no. 2185).*

A week has seven days, and each day has twenty-four hours. So how many hours of life do we have every week? God, our Creator, has given us all those hours in which to do many things, such as eating, sleeping, studying, playing games, texting, and watching television. Of all this time that is given to us, we are only required to spend one of those hours thanking and praising him: the hour spent celebrating Sunday Eucharist. Worship and resting on the first day of the week are so important and necessary for us that God gave us the Third Commandment.

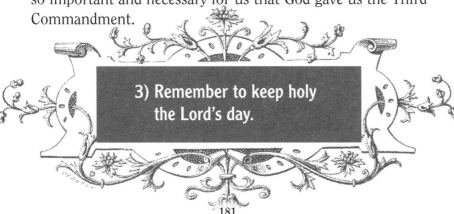

3) Remember to keep holy the Lord's day.

The observance of Sunday as a special day and a day of rest has a long history. In fact, it is rooted in Scripture's account of the dawn of creation.

The Sabbath

In Genesis, God made everything in six days and then rested on the seventh day. God also gave the Jewish people the seventh day, which was Saturday, as the Sabbath, a day of worship and rest. Jesus observed the Sabbath and declared himself Lord of the Sabbath.

Sunday as the Lord's Day

Sunday is truly the "day of the Sun"— Jesus, the Sun of Justice. Jesus rose from the dead on the first day of the week. So Christians observe Sunday, not Saturday, as the Lord's Day. It is the day of the new creation ushered in by the resurrection. On Sunday we praise our Creator and Redeemer in public worship. A precept of the Church requires us to keep the Lord's Day by participating in Mass.

BTW

Have you ever had a hard time getting to Mass because of a sports event or because your family was traveling? Check out www.masstimes.org to find Mass wherever you are.

Did You Know?

Every Sunday is a "little Easter," a celebration of Christ's resurrection.

BTW

The United States bishops allow the Solemnity of Mary, the Assumption, and the Feast of All Saints to be celebrated on Sunday when they fall on a Saturday or Monday. Most dioceses celebrate the Ascension on Sunday.

The Sunday Eucharist

The Eucharist, the celebration of the paschal mystery, is the heart of our Christian lives. For this reason, for Catholics all over the world, Sunday is a **holy day of obligation**. This means we are obliged to attend Mass on this day. Here are other holy days of obligation observed in the United States:

✦ The Solemnity of Mary, January 1

✦ The Ascension, fortieth day after Easter

✦ The Assumption of Mary, August 15

✦ Feast of All Saints, November 1

✦ The Immaculate Conception, December 8

✦ The Birth of Our Lord, December 25

In Canada, there are two:

✦ The Solemnity of Mary, January 1

✦ The Birth of Our Lord, December 25

Praying by ourselves is good. But when we assemble to pray with others in our parish, we express our unity as the Body of Christ. We also give witness to our faith and strengthen one another.

Sometimes it may not seem very important to go to Mass on Sundays or holy days. There are many reasons we may feel or think this way. Some people say they don't go to Mass because they don't get anything out of it. They forget that the Mass is not for *getting* but for *giving* God praise. Some people point to those who go to Mass but don't live the Gospel. The Eucharist gives us the strength to overcome temptations and to live as followers of Jesus. It's up to us to cooperate

A Catholic VIP

St. Clare (1193–1253)

Clare was born into a wealthy family in Assisi, Italy. She was attracted to the lifestyle of St. Francis, who had given up everything to live for God. So Clare became the first Franciscan sister. Her religious community stayed in their convent, slept on the floor, went barefoot, and prayed much. They lived on donated food. One Christmas Eve, Clare was sick in bed. That night, however, she saw and heard the Mass as though she were present for it. Because of this miracle, St. Clare is the patron of television. We celebrate her feast on August 11.

with God as he works in our lives and to try to live our Christian vocations faithfully. Finally, some people claim that the Mass is boring. It's true that some music or homilies are more interesting than others. However, our participation in the Mass is always a priceless act of worship in the eyes of God our Father. In the Eucharist, we are united to Jesus as he offers his life for our redemption. It's how Jesus asked us to remember him. In every Mass, God speaks to us and offers us himself.

Sunday Rest

The Third Commandment further obliges us to rest on Sunday. We need time to worship God and experience the joy that should characterize the Lord's Day. Sometimes a person's job may require work on a Sunday. People who really need to work are excused from the obligation of Sunday rest. They are encouraged, however, to worship another day.

Here are some ways to make Sunday holy:

Spend extra time in prayer.

Lend a hand to someone who needs help.

Enjoy God's creation by walking, hiking, swimming, sledding, or doing other outdoor activities.

Do something together with your family.

Exercise or play a game.

Learn something new.

Brainstorm

What is the value of having a day of rest each week? What does your family do to make Sunday special? What could you do to make it more special?

Scripture Link

A Sabbath Cure

Jesus often healed people on the Sabbath. This angered the religious leaders who thought healing on the Sabbath was forbidden because it was work. One day Jesus was teaching in the synagogue. A woman there had been stooped over for eighteen years. Jesus called her over and said, "You are healed!" He laid hands on her and she straightened up. The synagogue leader then told people not to come for cures on the Sabbath. Jesus asked the leaders if they untied their ox or donkey and led it to water on the Sabbath. He asked, "Shouldn't a daughter of Abraham be set free then?" The Sabbath is a day precisely for bringing about both spiritual and physical new life.

(cf. Lk 13:10–17)

From My Heart

Look at a picture or statue of the crucifixion. Thank Jesus for offering his life on Calvary and at every Mass. Ask him for the grace to participate in every Sunday Eucharist with all your heart.

Now Act!

Before you go to Mass,
read the readings and think
about what God is saying
to you.

Recap

• The Third Commandment tells us to observe the Lord's Day
and follow the example of God who rested after six days
of creating.

• For Christians, the Lord's Day is Sunday because Jesus rose
on this day.

• We make Sunday holy by celebrating the Eucharist
and by refraining from work.

• Sunday is also a day for extra prayer, doing things with the
family, and performing works of mercy.

Who Deserves Our Respect and Obedience?

33

Catechism *The Fourth Commandment tells us to honor and respect our parents as well as all those to whom God has given authority (cf. no. 2197).*

Each of us came into life as an infant. No creature is as helpless as a human baby. He or she cannot sit, stand, or even drink without help. For many years a child is very dependent on his or her parents. A child gradually matures and can live independently of parents or guardians. God has entrusted children to the loving care of parents for their instruction and for their protection. God, our heavenly Father, gave us the Fourth Commandment for our well-being:

4) Honor your father and your mother.

Authority from God

Just as God rules and guides the universe he created, all true authority on earth comes from God. People who are in positions of power have a responsibility to serve with justice. We are called to obey those in authority over us as long as what they tell us is in line with God's commands. We are not, of course, to follow laws and commands that would have us do something wrong. God's law and our conscience are always our guides.

Did You Know?

The Fourth Commandment is the only one with a promise attached. Scripture says, "Honor your father and your mother, . . . so that your days may be long and that it may go well with you" (Deut 5:16).

Honoring Parents

Just as your parents or those who care for you have obligations to you; to give you food, clothing, shelter, and an education; teach you how to live; and hand the faith on to you; you also have an obligation to them. The commandment to honor your mother and father means that you are to respect and love them. This includes obeying their rules. God asks us all to honor our parents, even when this is difficult.

After children grow up and leave home, they should still respect and love their parents. As parents age, the children become responsible for their care. This means visiting them, providing support, and helping them when they are sick.

Families

God created families for the good of their members, and society as a whole. A thriving society is founded on healthy families. Within the family we are all meant to learn how to love and become holy. This is possible because in the day-to-day challenges of family life, every family member is called on to share, sacrifice, and forgive.

Brainstorm

What are some rules in your family? How are they helpful?

What are some civil laws? How might they contribute to a peaceful, just society?

A Catholic VIP

St. Charles Lwanga (1860?–1886)

Charles Lwanga was a young page, a servant, in the court of King Mwanga in Uganda, Africa. He was known for being a good wrestler. Because Charles was also a good leader, he was put in charge of the pages. The king sometimes tempted Charles and the other pages to do sinful things, but Charles knew better than to obey him. Although the king was persecuting Christians, Charles was baptized along with other royal servants. He himself baptized five other pages who were drawn to Jesus. Their faith in Jesus cost these Christians their lives. We celebrate the feast of the twenty-two Ugandan martyrs on June 3.

Honoring Others

The Fourth Commandment also teaches us to honor our elders, especially older relatives. We are to obey any rightful authority, such as teachers, police officers, and civil leaders. We must follow the laws that govern our lives and ensure everyone's safety and security. We must be good citizens and help build a society of truth, justice, and freedom. Respect for authority brings about peace.

Gifts of Obedience

Obedience is good for us. It sets us free from selfishness and develops self-control. By obeying, we imitate Jesus who did his heavenly Father's will and also obeyed his parents on earth.

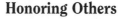

Scripture Link

Paying Taxes

Jesus is Lord of all, yet he was obedient. Scripture says that in Nazareth, Jesus obeyed Mary and Joseph. At the wedding in Cana, he listened to his mother's request. From the cross, he made sure that John would take care of her. Jesus also obeyed religious and civil law. One time, tax collectors asked Peter if Jesus paid the temple tax. Peter replied yes. Jesus told Peter to go to the sea to fish and take the first fish he hooked. In its mouth he would find a coin to pay the tax for both of them.

(cf. Mt 17:24–27)

From My Heart

In the garden the night before he died, Jesus prayed, "Father, not my will but yours be done" (Lk 22:42). Think a while about the obedience of Jesus in coming to earth and dying for us. Ask him to help you to do the right thing.

Now Act!

Plan to do something with your family for an elderly person or a person in need.

Recap

• **The Fourth Commandment tells us to honor and obey our mothers and fathers.**

• **All true authority comes from God.**

• **We are bound to obey people in authority and follow laws as long as they are in line with God's laws and our conscience.**

• **Families are meant to be where we learn to love and to be holy.**

34

Why Do We Respect Life?

Catechism *Life is sacred because God is the creator and the Lord of life (cf. no. 2258).*

Pizza, music, sunsets, Christmas, friends, sports. Life is beautiful! It offers many wonderful experiences to enjoy. Life is our most precious gift. Likewise, it is the greatest gift that others possess. God is the author of all life and the only one who has the right to determine how long someone will live. God made us in his image and likeness, sharing his life with us. Moreover, Jesus shed his blood for everyone. Therefore all people are sacred and have the right to life. To deliberately harm or destroy someone else's life is a serious sin. It is putting oneself in God's place. God's Fifth Commandment protects life:

5) You shall not kill.

Sins Against Life

All killing is wrong except in self-defense or in wars that are just. It is wrong to kill unborn babies **(abortion)**, for they have the right to life as much as any other human being. Putting people to death who are old or suffering **(euthanasia)** is also wrong, even though it may seem that relieving their misery is a good thing. Likewise, taking one's own life **(suicide)** is wrong. Because we don't know what was in their hearts, we leave people who commit suicide to the mercy of God.

Hatred is directly opposed to God's great law of love. Jesus said, "Love one another as I have loved you" (Jn 15:12). A Christian does not wish evil on others nor try to get revenge. Jesus said, "Love your enemies and pray for those who persecute you" (Mt 5:44). Anger is an emotion that is not wrong in itself. Anger becomes a sin when it leads to hatred, violence, or destructive behavior. Fighting, cruel words, grudges, **prejudice** (dislike of a certain group of people), and hurtful criticism are other sins against the Fifth Commandment. Jesus wants us to promote the kingdom of peace, justice, and love. Like him we must treat all people with respect, kindness, and compassion.

War is accompanied by evils, injustices, and suffering, and should be avoided if at all possible. We are all called to work and pray for peace. Those who serve their countries in the armed forces intend to work for peace by helping to keep nations safe and free. When efforts to make peace have failed, however, nations have the right to self-defense in order to protect the common good.

Did You Know? The Church teaches that capital punishment (the death penalty) is not the best response to serious crimes because it answers violence with more violence.

A Catholic VIP

Blessed Teresa of Calcutta (1910–1997)

Mother Teresa was known and admired worldwide for showing God's love to the poorest of the poor. Born to an Albanian family in what is now Macedonia, Mother Teresa joined the Sisters of Loreto, hoping to be a missionary in India. After teaching for several years in India, she felt God calling her to more directly serve the poor. She valued every life—poor people dying on the streets of India and babies whom no one wanted. She began a community, the Missionaries of Charity, and opened both a home for the dying and a children's home. Soon the Missionaries of Charity were working in more than a hundred countries. In 1979, Mother Teresa was awarded the Nobel Peace Prize.

Scandal

When we see someone doing good, we are motivated to do good too. The opposite may also be true. A person can lead someone into sin by giving a bad example. This is called giving **scandal**. Scandal comes from a Greek word that means a "trap" or a "stumbling block." Causing scandal harms a person's own spiritual life as well as the spiritual life of the other person. Older brothers and sisters need to be careful how they influence their younger siblings.

BTW

One of the corporal works of mercy is burying or showing respect for the dead.

Love for Self

We show we are grateful for the gift of our life by protecting it. This means we eat healthy foods, exercise, and get enough sleep. We avoid anything that endangers our lives, such as drugs, alcohol, smoking, reckless behavior, or joining gangs. We are careful not to injure ourselves. We also take good care of our spiritual life!

BTW

The people whose lives we can nurture or harm most easily are family members. Always show love and respect to family and friends.

Promoting Life

God calls us to protect and promote the life and dignity of all people. For example, we help provide material goods like food, clothing, and shelter for those who have less than we do. We also support people by giving them encouragement, sympathy, and understanding. We show love for God by respecting his creatures and by taking care of our pets.

Brainstorm

What are some words that show that you value life?

Scripture Link

Reconciliation

Jesus, the Prince of Peace, taught, "When you are offering your gift at the altar, if you remember that your brother or sister has something against you, leave your gift there before the altar and go; first be reconciled to your brother or sister, and then come and offer your gift." Another time, Peter asked how often he should forgive someone. Jesus replied, "Seventy-seven times." This was his way of saying, "Always."

(cf. Mt 5:23–24; 18:21–22)

From My Heart

Lord, make me an instrument of your peace.
Where there is hatred, let me sow love;
Where there is injury, pardon;
Where there is doubt, faith;
Where there is despair, hope;
Where there is darkness, light;
Where there is sadness, joy.

O, Divine Master, grant that I may not so much seek to be
consoled, as to console; to be understood, as to understand;
to be loved, as to love; for it is in giving that we receive, it is
in pardoning that we are pardoned, it is in dying that we are
born to eternal life.

Now Act!

Start a habit to improve your life
such as eating healthy food, going to
bed on time, or getting exercise outside.

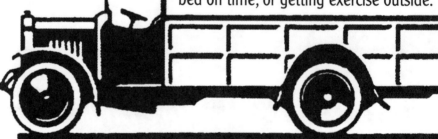

Recap

- **The Fifth Commandment tells us to respect life by protecting
  our own life and promoting the lives of others.**

- **God is the author of life, and he alone has the right to decide
  when it will end.**

- **Killing, fighting, hatred, and scandal are sins against the Fifth
  Commandment.**

Why Did God Make Us Male and Female?

35

Catechism *God made men and women to experience a loving communion and to add new members to the human race (cf. no. 2331).*

The love that a husband and wife promise to each other is different from the love they give anyone else. When friends make promises to each other, both are expected to keep them. If two friends, for example, promise to go to a party together and one of them doesn't show up, the trust they had is broken. Imagine what it's like then when a married person is not faithful to his or her wife or husband. That is why God gave us the following two commandments to protect marriage and to keep our hearts pure.

6) You shall not commit adultery.

9) You shall not covet your neighbor's wife. (**Covet** means to want for oneself something that belongs to another.)

Honoring the Image of God in Ourselves and Others

When God created us in his image, he made us male and female. **Sexuality** is the gift of being either male or female. All of us reflect God's image, but in different ways. Some of us reflect the divine image by our strength, some by tenderness. Some reflect it by being protective and others by being nurturing. Some reflect God's image in their creativity and some reflect it by appreciating others. Some of these characteristics are physical. God made our bodies in such a way that we can show love with them. In particular, men and women who are married express the deep love they have for one another through sex. This gives them great joy. Through this special act of love a husband and wife cooperate with God and give birth to new life in their children. Married couples use their gift of love to serve God.

People who respect themselves and others do not abuse the gift of sexuality. They share this gift with their marriage partner as a sign of lifelong love. Being unfaithful leads to unhappiness. It harms our relationships with God and others.

Power of Love

Sexuality is a powerful force because it is linked to life and love. It can be misused or threatened in ways that show little respect for ourselves and others, as well as little love for God.

The gift of sex belongs to marriage. To make use of the special love of a marriage when we are not married is wrong. It is disrespectful of God's Sixth Commandment. It is also disrespectful toward one's partner and the children who may be born.

Adultery means sharing this special married love with someone who is not one's marriage partner. It is a serious sin. Broken marriage vows cause pain not only to the spouses, but to their children and to society.

Pornography is sex-related pictures or text in magazines or on the Internet. Viewing pornography tears down a healthy attitude toward sexuality.

While we treat all people with care and respect, we believe that **homosexual acts** are wrong because they disregard God's plan of love between a man and a woman.

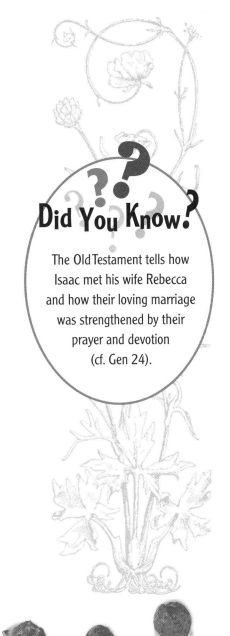

Did You Know?

The Old Testament tells how Isaac met his wife Rebecca and how their loving marriage was strengthened by their prayer and devotion
(cf. Gen 24).

A Catholic VIP

St. Maria Goretti
(1890–1902)

Maria belonged to a poor farming family in Italy. After her father died, her family shared a house with another family. This family's eighteen-year-old son, Alessandro, read books and kept pictures that led him to sin. When Maria was twelve and alone in the house, he tried to abuse her. When Maria resisted him, Alessandro stabbed her many times. Before she died the next day, Maria forgave Alessandro and prayed for him. While he was in prison Maria appeared to him in a dream and gave him lilies. After twenty-seven years, he was released and entered a monastery to do penance. St. Maria Goretti's feast day is July 6.

The Virtue of Chastity

The virtue of **chastity** means different things depending on one's vocation. Married people are chaste when they give themselves only to their marriage partner. Single people are chaste by not expressing to others the special love that exists only between married partners. Those people who are consecrated to God as priests or religious are chaste by preserving their hearts for Jesus alone.

Movies, books, and songs do not always reflect God's view of marriage. They might make sins against love and chastity attractive. Practicing chastity requires strength. We become strong through self-control, by not always doing what we feel like doing.

Tips for Chastity

As you grow older, it will be more challenging to resist temptation and practice chastity. Here are some ways to grow strong:

1. Pray, especially to our heavenly mother Mary, who is called All-Pure.

2. Choose books, music, movies, and websites wisely.

3. Learn about the saints and other good people.

4. Pick friends who are good and kind.

5. Celebrate the Eucharist and receive Holy Communion frequently.

6. Receive the sacrament of Penance often.

7. When we have questions, ask a well-informed adult.

Treasuring Sexuality

When we view sexuality as God sees it, we respect our bodies. God dwells in us and so we are temples of God. We show respect for our bodies by what we wear, what we listen to and watch, what we say, and what we do. We insult the dignity of our bodies by telling what are called "dirty" jokes or using language that cheapens sex or makes fun of our bodies. We should avoid listening to songs and watching movies that disrespect sex. If we do these things, then we will have pure hearts. We will show that we are grateful to God for our bodies and for his gift of love.

Friendship

Couples who are best friends have solid marriages. We can prepare to be a good husband or wife by being a good friend. We ask: Can I sacrifice something to make a friend happy? Can I be a giver instead of a taker? We can also prepare for a good marriage by learning how to choose good friends.

BTW

"Blessed are the pure in heart, for they will see God" —Jesus (Mt 5:8).

Brainstorm

What qualities do you want in a friend?

Scripture Link

True Love

True love lasts. The Song of Solomon (also called Song of Songs) is a book in the Bible that celebrates love. It says, "Many waters cannot quench love, neither can floods drown it" (Song 8:7). The love between a man and a woman that is sealed by marriage vows is meant to last.

From My Heart

Loving Father, thank you for
creating each of us in your image.
Help us to honor your image in ourselves
and in others. You sent your Son, Jesus,
to be our example. Teach us how to be
faithful, to keep the promises we make,
and to live with pure hearts, so that
we may see you face to face.
Amen.

Now Act!

Make a list of rules
for friends to follow in
order to stay friends.

Recap

• •

- **Sexuality is the gift of being male or female.**

- **Through sex, a married couple expresses their special love and can cooperate with God in creating new human beings.**

- **Sharing with another person the special love that was promised to a husband or wife is the serious sin of adultery.**

- **Because we are made in God's image and are temples of God, we show respect for our sexuality and our bodies.**

- **We show respect for ourselves and others when we are chaste.**

What Is Involved in Honesty?

36

Catechism *The Seventh Commandment forbids stealing or harming what belongs to another. It requires that we care for the goods of the earth and share them (cf. no. 2401).*

Robin Hood and his merry men stole from the rich and gave to the poor. This sounds like a noble thing to do, but when something is wrong, doing it is wrong, even if the intention is good. Stealing is wrong. Why? Stealing disrespects another person's right to own property. We know how it hurts when something is stolen from us. It shakes our trust in other people. To protect us from the injustice of robbery, God gave us two commandments. One forbids stealing, and the other forbids even the desire to possess what belongs to another person. These commandments are all about respect: respect for people and respect for the gifts of this world.

> 7) You shall not steal.
>
> 10) You shall not covet your neighbor's goods.

A Catholic VIP

St. Vincent de Paul (1580–1660)

As a priest, St. Vincent de Paul was chaplain to the French queen and lived a life of luxury. One day a sermon inspired him to begin his life's work of caring for those in need. He organized groups to distribute food and clothing. Eventually Vincent started a religious order of priests who preached to the poor and helped prisoners and slaves. He also involved wealthy people in helping others. With the help of St. Louise de Marillac, Vincent founded a woman's religious community called the Daughters of Charity. Today his name and work live on in the religious communities he founded and in St. Vincent de Paul Societies. St. Vincent's feast day is September 27.

The Lure of Wealth

Some people may want to win the lottery or earn a large salary. They think that having a lot of money and possessions will make them happy. This isn't really true. There are other people who are as stingy as the miser Scrooge in Dickens' book *A Christmas Carol*. In the First Letter to Timothy in the New Testament, we are warned that the love of money is a source of much evil. It can lead people to steal and cheat. Jesus told a parable about a man whose crops were abundant, much more than he needed. Instead of sharing his blessings with others, he decided to build bigger barns to store his harvest. That night he died. What good was his wealth to him then?

BTW

In Matthew's Gospel Jesus says: "It is easier for a camel to go through the eye of a needle than for someone who is rich to enter the kingdom of God" (Mt 19:24).

Honesty

Justice means giving every person what he or she deserves. It requires that we are honest with each other. Here are some ways to be honest and avoid taking what does not belong to us:

- If a clerk gives us too much change, we return it.

- If we can see someone's test paper, we don't steal his or her answers.

- If we sell something, we ask a fair price.

- If we borrow something, we return it.

- If we damage something that belongs to others, we offer to fix it or pay for it.

- If we find something, we try to find its owner.

- If others work for us, we pay them a fair wage. On the other hand, if we work for others, we do a good job.

Shoplifting is stealing. It is also against the Seventh Commandment to accept or buy anything that was stolen. Gambling in moderation isn't wrong unless a person wastes money that should be used to provide for his or her family.

Did You Know?

Plagiarizing (PLAY-juh-rise-ing) or copying work that is created by someone else without giving them credit for it, is also stealing. So is cheating on a test.

BTW

Using God's gifts in the right way includes being kind to animals. On the other hand, it is wrong to pour out on them money and affection that should be spent on people.

The World Belongs to All

God gave the world to everyone. We are all responsible for it. This is why it is wrong to damage and destroy public places or leave litter. Neither do we waste water and electricity or destroy forests and wildlife. By taking care of the world, we provide for future generations.

People who are wealthy have a duty to share what they have with the poor. Likewise, wealthy nations are to take responsibility to assist nations that are developing. Jesus said that anyone who feeds the hungry or clothes the naked does so to him. When our needs are provided for, we should be satisfied with what we have and not be envious of what others have. **Envy** is sadness because someone else has good things and we want to have them for ourselves.

Jesus taught the Church to have special love for people who do not have the basic necessities of life and dignity. The **works of mercy** are acts by which we aid the poor. Spiritual works of mercy focus on people's spirit, while corporal works of mercy help their bodies. See what these are on page 229.

Did You Know?

Solidarity is a Christian virtue. It is to recognize that all members of the human race are bound together as one family and are responsible for one another.

Brainstorm

What organizations help provide food, shelter, clothing, and the like for those who need assistance? How could you help them?

Giving Back What Is Not Ours

Zacchaeus was a tax collector who cheated people. One day he wanted to see Jesus, who was passing by. But Zacchaeus was too short to see over the crowd. So he ran ahead and climbed a sycamore tree. When Jesus got to the spot, he called out, "Zacchaeus, come down. I will have supper at your house today." Zacchaeus quickly came out of the tree. People grumbled, "How can Jesus eat with him, a sinner?" Then Zacchaeus promised to give back four times what he had stolen (cf. Lk 19:1–10).

Paying back is called **restitution** (res-ti-TOO-shuhn). If we have stolen something, we must make our best effort to return what was stolen, or in some way repair the damage we have done. If this isn't possible, money can be donated to a church or charitable organization instead.

Scripture Link

Jesus told the parable about Lazarus, a starving man covered with sores, who lay at a rich man's door every day. Lazarus longed to eat just the crumbs from the rich man's table, but the rich man never noticed him. Lazarus died and went to rest with Abraham in peace. The rich man died and went to a place of torment and flames. He cried out to Abraham to let Lazarus dip his finger in water and come to cool his tongue. But Abraham said, "No." Then the rich man pleaded, "Send Lazarus to warn my five brothers so they won't end up here with me." But Abraham said, "If they don't listen to Moses and the prophets, they won't listen even if someone rises from the dead." Jesus told this story to teach us that we should be aware of the needs of those around us.

(cf. Lk 16:19–31)

From My Heart

Dear Jesus, teach me how to be generous, not selfish. Help me be giving, not greedy. Show me how to care for and protect the things of this world, not damage or destroy them. Help me be charitable, not unjust. I want to hear the cry of the poor and be like you.

Now Act!

Aim to do a corporal work of mercy by donating clothes and toys that you don't use to a charitable organization. Take up a collection or carry out a project to raise money for the needy.

Recap

- **The Seventh and Tenth Commandments protect people's right to own property.**

- **They tell us to respect others' property by not taking or damaging it and to be just in our dealings with others.**

- **We are to take care of the goods of the earth and to share them with others, especially those in need.**

- **We are not to envy others.**

Why Is Truth Important?

Catechism *People owe one another the truth, which makes it possible to live together in peace (cf. no. 2469).*

Remember the story of the boy who cried, "Wolf"? He called it so often as a prank that when a wolf really came and he cried, "Wolf!" the villagers ignored him. Society only runs well if we can trust one another. This trust is like glue that holds us together. Truthfulness builds the trust necessary for relationships and community. Lies cause confusion and trouble. They can also hurt people.

We have a right to know the truth. To safeguard this right, God gave us this commandment:

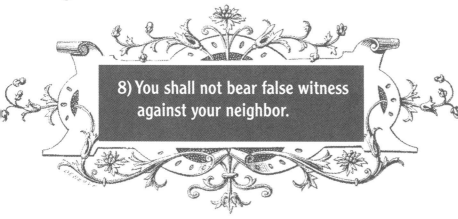

8) You shall not bear false witness against your neighbor.

Bearing false witness means claiming that untrue information about a person is true. This is especially serious in court when a person's future may depend on someone telling the truth. Lying after taking an oath to tell the truth is the crime of **perjury**. When Jesus was captured and taken before the authorities, some men falsely claimed that he had said and done things against the law. They bore false witness against Jesus.

Did You Know?

Jesus said, "I am the way, and the truth, and the life" (Jn 14:6). The closer we are to the truth, the closer we are to him!

BTW

Through the arts we are able to express the truth in the languages of sight, sound, and symbol. When we create, we are imitating God the Creator.

Brainstorm

Why do you think people lie? How can one lie lead to other sins?

The Value of Truth

Lying is saying what is not true with the intent of deceiving someone. White lies and fibs are still lies and are wrong. It is also wrong to withhold information, tell a partial truth, or exaggerate. One of the greatest insults is to be called a liar. On the other hand, we like to be known as truthful persons. We value truth. Truthfulness is a sign of a good character.

Other Ways to Treat the Truth

Breaking a promise is wrong. People trust us to keep our word. Also, telling a secret that someone confided to us or that we learn by accident is wrong. Professional people like doctors, lawyers, and counselors know things about people that are confidential. They are bound to keep certain information secret.

Some truths that are not to be kept secret are the truths of the faith. We Christians have a duty to witness to our faith by word and deed. Persons who bear the supreme witness of giving up their lives for their faith are called **martyrs** (MAR-ters). The word *martyr* is Greek for "witness."

Another sin against the Eighth Commandment is **rash judgment**. This means assuming that a person has sinned even though we have no evidence. We should always try to see the best in people and give them the benefit of the doubt, and hope they don't judge us harshly too!

Hypocrisy (hih-POK-rih-see) is another form of lying. This means pretending to have a good quality when we don't. For example, a girl lets everyone think she is kind to her little brother, but when they're alone, she is mean to him. Sometimes hypocrisy is saying one thing but doing another.

A Catholic VIP

St. Francis de Sales (1567–1622)

Francis came from a noble French family and studied to be a lawyer. His father wanted him to marry an heiress. Instead Francis became a priest and served in a town where people had left the Church. Besides preaching, Francis wrote and personally handed out beautiful explanations of the faith. Thousands of people returned to the Church. He became a bishop and wrote books and many letters teaching people that everyone can become holy. With St. Jane de Chantal, he founded the Sisters of the Visitation of Holy Mary. St. Francis is the patron of writers. His feast day is January 24.

Hateful Words

The Eighth Commandment also guards a person's good name, or reputation. It forbids **detraction**, which is speaking unnecessarily about the faults of others. It also forbids **calumny** (KAL-uhm-nee), which is saying untrue things about another person. In other words, we are to avoid gossip and spreading rumors.

St. Francis de Sales said we should imagine shaking a feather pillow in the wind and letting the feathers fly out. You would have a hard time getting them all back! This is what it's like when we harm someone's good name. It is difficult to repair the damage, but we are to try.

BTW

Gossip that is spread through texting or the Internet can be even more hurtful than unkind words spoken to another person because it can be seen by many people.

Truth Test

When to tell the truth is sometimes hard to know. For example, should I tell the truth if my friend will get into trouble, if it's a family secret, or if someone's feelings will be hurt? Two questions help us decide: Is it necessary? Is it kind? Some secrets that could be harmful to ourselves or others should be told to a trusted adult.

Media

People involved in communications media have a responsibility to present the truth to the best of their ability. However, they too must show respect for persons as they report the truth.

Scripture Link

Taming the Tongue

St. James wrote about the power of speech. He compared it to the strength of a horse, which must be bridled, or to a ship that needs to be controlled by a rudder. James also said that the tongue is like fire that can set a great forest ablaze. He warned against using the tongue to bless God and then to curse people.

(cf. Jas 3:3–12)

From My Heart

Think about times when it is hard for you to tell the truth. Think about times when you've spoken about the faults of others. Ask the Holy Spirit to give you the courage and strength to be more like Jesus.

Learn something about a Christian martyr who died for the truth.

Now Act!

Recap

• The Eighth Commandment safeguards the truth, which makes it possible for people to live peacefully with one another.

• We promote truth by avoiding lying, hypocrisy, rash judgment, detraction, and calumny.

• Being truthful means keeping promises as well as secrets.

• We are to bear witness to the truths of the faith.

What Is Prayer?

38

Catechism *Prayer is the lifting of our mind and heart to God. It is God's gift to us that builds our relationship with him (cf. nos. 2559, 2565).*

God always answers prayers. Sometimes he says yes. But sometimes God says no, or "wait a little," or "I have a better idea." Former U.S. president Jimmy Carter remarked that sometimes God says, "You've got to be kidding!" When we think of prayer, we usually think of asking for something. But prayer is much more than that. It is the raising of the mind and heart to God. Just thinking about God can be praying. If we love God, then we will pray, because in prayer we talk to God and listen to him. We may pray alone or with others. Our greatest prayer is the Eucharist, which we pray gathered together as God's people.

Some prayers, such as the Lord's Prayer and the Hail Mary, have been prayed by Catholics for centuries. Knowing these prayers lets us pray together easily. These prayers, as well as other prayers people have composed, can express for us what is in our hearts. But there are many more ways to pray. As you grow, your ways of praying will probably change.

215

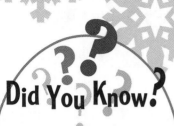

Did You Know?

Jesus said whatever we ask for in his name we will receive. That is why many prayers end in a phrase like "through Jesus Christ our Lord."

Kinds of Prayer

Prayer can be vocal (aloud) or mental (only in your mind). Thinking about God, something Jesus did or said, or a truth of our faith is called **meditation**. You can even meditate on a religious picture. Another form of prayer is **contemplation**, in which no words are used. We just enjoy God's presence, loving him and being loved by him. Silence helps us listen to God and focus our attention on him.

The psalms, or song-prayers, in the Bible are a special kind of prayer. We pray a psalm at every Mass, and many of our hymns are based on psalms. Also, each hour of the Liturgy of the Hours includes a psalm or two.

Finally, we can always talk to God in our own words, sharing with him whatever is on our mind or in our heart.

BTW

Prayers that are repeated over a period of days have special names. A **Triduum** is three days of prayer. An **octave** (OK-tiv) is eight days of prayer. A **novena** (noh-VEE-nuh) is nine days of prayer.

Purposes of Prayer

1. *Blessing* or *adoration*. We bless or adore God because he is our almighty Creator. At Mass we proclaim, "Blessed be God forever!" We bless God who blesses us with good things.

2. *Thanksgiving*. Everything we are and have comes from God, so we express our gratitude. Once when Jesus healed ten lepers and only one came back to thank him, he asked where the others were. God likes to be thanked as much as we do (cf. Lk 17:11-19).

3. *Petition*. Knowing God is all-powerful and all-loving, we ask him for what we need. Jesus told us, "Ask, and it will be given you; search, and you will find; knock, and the door will be opened for you" (Mt 7:7).

4. *Intercession*. We ask God to help other people, too. For example, at Mass we pray intercessions for the Church, for government officials, for people who are sick, and for those who have died.

5. *Praise*. God is amazing! We praise God for what he does, but beyond that we praise God with joy for who he is.

BTW

Days of recollection and retreats are times away from our everyday lives when we deepen our faith and pray more than usual.

A Catholic VIP

St. Rose Philippine Duchesne (1769–1852)

St. Rose from France joined a community of sisters called the Society of the Sacred Heart. With all her heart she hoped to bring Jesus to the native peoples of North America. Finally, she was sent to Missouri. There she opened convents and the first free school for girls west of the Mississippi. When she was seventy-one years old, she was allowed to go to Kansas to open a school for children of the Potawatomi tribe. St. Rose couldn't speak the language or teach, but she prayed so much that the Indians called her "Woman Who Always Prays." When she became ill, St. Rose returned to Missouri, where she devoted the rest of her life to prayer. St. Rose's feast day is November 18.

Jesus as Model

Jesus taught us how to pray by his word and example. He told us to ask our heavenly Father for things and advised us to pray with faith and humility. Jesus himself prayed before major events in his life, such as choosing the apostles, raising Lazarus from the dead, and being crucified. He prayed alone and with others. Sometimes Jesus prayed all night!

Did You Know?

How do you know if you are praying well? One test is whether you are doing what God tells us to do in the Ten Commandments.

Time and Place

We are encouraged to pray first thing in the morning, before we go to bed, and before and after meals. Anytime, though, is a good time to pray. We can say short prayers while we are waiting for something to download or when we're standing in line. We can also pray in any place, but it helps to have a favorite, quiet spot. You might set up a prayer corner with a Bible and a religious picture or statue that you like.

Sometimes when we try to pray, we get distracted. Our mind jumps to other ideas. We can weave these stray thoughts into our prayer. For example, if we're worried about a test, we can pray, "Holy Spirit, help me do well on the test."

Brainstorm

What are your favorite prayers? How do you like to pray?

Lectio Divina

Lectio divina is Latin for "sacred reading." It is a way of getting in touch with God that has been practiced for centuries. You might like to try this four-step prayer.

1. Read a passage from Scripture until a word or phrase catches your attention.

2. Think about why that word or phrase jumped out at you.

3. When you realize what the word means for you, respond to God about it. You might pray words of praise, thanks, contrition, petition, or love.

4. Sit silently in God's presence.

Scripture Link

Never Give Up

Jesus taught us to persevere in prayer through two parables. In one, a woman kept asking a judge to hear her case. He gives in just so that she will stop pestering him. In another parable, a man has a visitor at midnight but has nothing to feed him. So he goes to his neighbor whose family is sleeping and pounds on his door. Although the neighbor at first tells him to go away, he finally gets up and gives the persistent man bread. In both of these stories, the people received what they needed because they didn't give up.

(cf. Lk 11:5–8; 18:1–8)

Make your own prayer book including a collection of prayers you like or wrote.

Now Act!

Ask three people to tell you their favorite way to pray.

From My Heart

One thing we can pray for is the grace to pray well. Ask the Holy Spirit to make you a person of prayer.

Recap

- **Prayer is the raising of the mind and heart to God.**

- **Prayer can be vocal or mental and carried out alone or with others.**

- **The five purposes of prayer are blessing, thanksgiving, petition, intercession, and praise.**

- **Some forms of prayer are meditation, contemplation, singing or reciting psalms, and *lectio divina*.**

What Does the Our Father Really Mean?

Catechism *In the Our Father we first focus on God's glory and pray that his name be made holy, that his kingdom come, and that his will be carried out. Then we present our needs to God, praying that we may be nourished and forgiven, and may triumph over evil (cf. no. 2857).*

When people are preparing to become Catholic, they are presented with the Our Father prayer. This prayer was originally a gift that Jesus gave to his followers. One day the apostles asked Jesus to teach them how to pray, and he taught them the Our Father. That is why this prayer is also called the Lord's Prayer. The first Christians prayed the Our Father three times a day. Today we pray it at Mass, in the Divine Office, in the Rosary, the Divine Mercy chaplet, and at other times. We can pray the Lord's Prayer any time.

"...teach us to pray..."

"When you pray say 'Our Father, who art in heaven...'"

What the Prayer Means

The Our Father has seven petitions. The first three are about God; the last four are about our needs. Let's look at what the words of this prayer mean.

Our Father—We address God as Father, just as Jesus did. Jesus called God "Abba," and God is our "Abba," too. He is not a force or a cold, impersonal, almighty being, but our Father, the one who created us and loves us. At Baptism, we became God's adopted children. As children of God, we are a family, bound together as brothers and sisters. That is why we pray "our" Father and not just "my" Father.

Who art in heaven—Heaven is wherever God is. It is the destiny God intends for us.

Hallowed be thy name—*Hallowed* means "holy." So in this phrase we praise God by declaring that he is holy. We pray that everyone live in a way that glorifies God.

Thy kingdom come—God's kingdom is characterized by justice and peace. In God's kingdom, all people live in love; there are no enemies. We pray that this kingdom, begun by Jesus, may come in its fullness, and we wait for the Lord's return at the end of time.

Thy will be done on earth as it is in heaven—In the kingdom of heaven, saints and angels serve and honor God with great joy. We pray that people on earth also serve and honor God, so that we can experience the peace and joy of God's kingdom. Jesus and Mary show us how to live according to God's will.

Give us this day our daily bread—Aware that all good gifts come from God, we ask him to give us what we need each day. Bread also refers both to the Word of God, which nourishes us, and to the sacred Bread of the Eucharist. This petition makes the Our Father a good prayer to pray before meals.

And forgive us our trespasses as we forgive those who trespass against us—We should pay close attention when we pray this. *Trespasses* is another word for sins. We ask God to forgive our sins in the same way that we are willing to forgive others, even our enemies.

And lead us not into temptation—Temptations are pressures or urges to sin. People, places, and things can tempt us or lead us into sin. We ask God to strengthen and protect us from these.

But deliver us from evil—We ask God to save us from all evil and the Evil One, Satan. Then we will belong to God's kingdom and live in perfect joy forever.

Doxology

The Gospel of Matthew has a prayer of praise at the end of the Our Father: **For the kingdom, the power and the glory are yours, now and forever**. Catholics don't add this to the prayer as other Christians often do, but it is prayed in the Mass shortly after the Our Father.

BTW

The Our Father sums up the whole Gospel.

A Catholic VIP

A Catholic VIP

St. Teresa of Avila (1515–1582)

Teresa was a lively, attractive girl from a wealthy family in Avila, Spain. When she was twenty, she joined the Carmelites. After eighteen years, Teresa received the grace of a deeper prayer life. She felt God calling her to reform the Carmelites. First she founded a stricter order of nuns called the Discalced, or "barefoot," Carmelites. These nuns slept on straw mats and didn't eat meat. Then Teresa and St. John of the Cross, a Carmelite who was inspired by her example, founded the male branch of the Discalced Carmelites. Teresa's written works have helped others grow closer to God for centuries. She was the first woman to be named a doctor of the Church. Her feast day is October 15.

The Best Prayer

Blessed Pope John XXIII said that knowing the Our Father and putting it into practice is living the Christian life. In teaching about prayer, St. Teresa of Avila declared that the Our Father could lead to the highest form of prayer and union with God. She recommended praying the Our Father very slowly.

BTW

During the Middle Ages, when not everyone could read, many people who couldn't pray the 150 psalms in the Liturgy of the Hours prayed 150 Our Fathers in Latin instead. They prayed on beads called paternosters.

Brainstorm

Name three qualities of God that make him a good father. What line of the Our Father means the most to you?

Scripture Link

The Agony in the Garden

The night before he died, Jesus took his apostles to a garden. He told them to wait while he prayed. He went apart, and, dreading what was coming, prayed, "My Father, if it is possible, let this cup pass from me; yet not what I want but what you want." This is the way we should pray, always adding, "If it is your will," because our heavenly Father knows best.

(cf. Mt 26:3–39)

Did You Know?

On the Mount of Olives near Jerusalem, is the Church of the Pater Noster (which is Latin for "Our Father"). On its courtyard walls are ceramic plaques with the Our Father in most languages of the world, including Braille.

From My Heart

Pray a litany of thanksgiving for all that the Father has given you. Name things you are grateful for and after each one respond, "I thank you, Father."

Now Act!

Find examples of how God's kingdom is coming about by people working for justice and peace. This can be done in big ways and little ways. Pray the Our Father for them.

Recap

- Jesus gave us the Our Father.

- In the first part of the Our Father after declaring that God is holy, we pray that his kingdom may come in its fullness and that his will may be done.

- In the second part of the Our Father we ask for what we need, for forgiveness, and for protection from evil.

Appendixes

1. How Catholics Live

The Ten Commandments

1. I am the Lord your God: you shall not have other gods besides me.

2. You shall not take the name of the Lord your God in vain.

3. Remember to keep holy the Lord's day.

4. Honor your father and your mother.

5. You shall not kill.

6. You shall not commit adultery.

7. You shall not steal.

8. You shall not bear false witness against your neighbor.

9. You shall not covet your neighbor's wife.

10. You shall not covet your neighbor's goods.

Duties of Catholics (Precepts of the Church)

1. To attend Mass on Sundays and holy days of obligation.

2. To receive the sacrament of Reconciliation at least once a year.

3. To receive Holy Communion during the Easter Season.

4. To observe the days of fast and abstinence.

5. To strengthen and support the Church.

The Beatitudes

Blessed are the poor in spirit, for theirs is the
kingdom of heaven.

Blessed are they who mourn, for they shall be
comforted.

Blessed are the meek, for they shall possess
the earth.

Blessed are they who hunger and thirst for
justice, for they shall be satisfied.

Blessed are the merciful, for they shall obtain
mercy.

Blessed are the pure of heart, for they shall
see God.

Blessed are the peacemakers, for they shall be
called children of God.

Blessed are they who suffer persecution
for righteousness' sake, for theirs is
the kingdom of heaven.

Corporal Works of Mercy

Feed the hungry.

Give drink to the thirsty.

Clothe the naked.

Visit the sick.

Shelter the homeless.

Visit the imprisoned.

Bury the dead.

Spiritual Works of Mercy

Admonish the sinner.

Instruct the ignorant.

Counsel the doubtful.

Comfort the afflicted.

Bear wrongs patiently.

Forgive injuries.

Pray for the living
and the dead.

Theological Virtues

Faith

Hope

Charity

Cardinal Moral Virtues

Prudence

Justice

Fortitude

Temperance

Gifts of the Holy Spirit

Wisdom

Understanding

Counsel (Right Judgment)

Fortitude (Courage)

Knowledge

Piety (Love)

Fear of the Lord (Reverence)

Fruits of the Holy Spirit

Charity   Generosity

Joy   Gentleness

Peace   Faithfulness

Patience   Modesty

Kindness   Self-control

Goodness   Chastity

2. How Catholics Pray

The Sign of the Cross

Catholics usually begin and end prayers with the Sign of the Cross. As we pray it, we trace a cross over ourselves with our right hand, touching our forehead, chest, left and right shoulders.

In the name of the Father, (forehead)

and of the Son, (chest)

and of the Holy (left shoulder)

Spirit. (right shoulder)

Amen. (hands folded)

The Our Father

Our Father, who art in heaven, hallowed be thy name. Thy kingdom come, thy will be done on earth as it is in heaven. Give us this day our daily bread, and forgive us our trespasses as we forgive those who trespass against us. And lead us not into temptation, but deliver us from evil. Amen.

Hail Mary

Hail Mary, full of grace, the Lord is with you. Blessed are you among women and blessed is the fruit of your womb, Jesus. Holy Mary, Mother of God, pray for us sinners now and at the hour of our death. Amen.

Glory

Glory to the Father and to the Son and to the Holy Spirit. As it was in the beginning is now, and will be for ever. Amen.

The Apostles' Creed

Credo
in unum
Deum.

I believe in God,
the Father almighty,
Creator of heaven and earth,
and in Jesus Christ, his only Son, our Lord,
who was conceived by the Holy Spirit,
born of the Virgin Mary,
suffered under Pontius Pilate,
was crucified, died and was buried;
he descended into hell;
on the third day he rose again from the dead;
he ascended into heaven,
and is seated at the right hand of God the Father almighty;
from there he will come to judge the living and the dead.
I believe in the Holy Spirit,
the holy catholic Church,
the communion of saints,
the forgiveness of sins,
the resurrection of the body,
and life everlasting. Amen.

Act of Faith

O my God, I firmly believe that you are one God in three divine Persons, Father, Son, and Holy Spirit; I believe that your divine Son became man and died for our sins, and that he will come to judge the living and the dead. I believe these and all the truths which the Holy Catholic Church teaches, because you revealed them, who can neither deceive nor be deceived.

Act of Hope

O my God, relying on your infinite goodness and promises, I hope to obtain pardon of my sins, the help of your grace, and life everlasting, through the merits of Jesus Christ, my Lord and Redeemer.

Act of Love

O my God, I love you above all things, with my whole heart and soul, because you are all good and worthy of all my love. I love my neighbor as myself for the love of you. I forgive all who have injured me and I ask pardon of all whom I have injured.

Act of Contrition

My God, I am sorry for my sins with all my heart. In choosing to do wrong and failing to do good, I have sinned against you whom I should love above all things. I firmly intend, with your help, to do penance, to sin no more, and to avoid whatever leads me to sin. Our Savior Jesus Christ suffered and died for us. In his name, my God, have mercy.

For the Deceased

Eternal rest grant unto them,
   O Lord,
and let perpetual light shine
   upon them.
And may the souls of all the
   faithful departed,
through the mercy of God,
   rest in peace. Amen.

The Angelus

V. The Angel of the Lord declared unto Mary.

R. And she conceived of the Holy Spirit. (Hail Mary. . . .)

V. Behold the handmaid of the Lord.

R. Be it done unto me according to your word. (Hail Mary. . . .)

V. And the Word became Flesh.

R. And lived among us. (Hail Mary. . . .)

V. Pray for us, O Holy Mother of God.

R. That we may be made worthy of the promises of Christ.

Let us pray: O Lord, it was through the message of an angel that we learned of the Incarnation of your Son Christ. Pour your grace into our hearts, and by his passion and cross bring us to the glory of his resurrection. Through the same Christ our Lord. Amen.

Queen of Heaven (Regina Caeli)

(Said during the Easter Season instead of the Angelus)
Queen of heaven, rejoice. Alleluia.
For he whom you deserved to bear, Alleluia.
Has risen as he said, Alleluia.
Pray for us to God, Alleluia.

V. Rejoice and be glad, O Virgin Mary! Alleluia!

R. Because our Lord is truly risen, Alleluia.

Let us pray:
O God, by the resurrection of your Son, our Lord Jesus Christ, you have made glad the whole world. Grant, we pray, that, through the intercession of the Virgin Mary, his Mother, we may attain the joys of eternal life. Through Christ our Lord. Amen.

Memorare

Remember, O most gracious Virgin Mary, that never was it known that anyone who fled to your protection, implored your help, or sought your intercession, was left unaided. Inspired with this confidence, I fly to thee, O Virgin of virgins, my Mother; to you I come, before you I stand, sinful and sorrowful. O Mother of the Word Incarnate, despise not my petitions, but in your mercy hear and answer them. Amen.

Hail, Holy Queen (Salve Regina)

Hail, Holy Queen, Mother of Mercy, our life, our sweetness, and our hope! To you we cry, poor banished children of Eve; to you we send up our sighs, mourning and weeping in this valley of tears. Turn then, most gracious advocate, your eyes of mercy toward us, and after this our exile, show unto us the blessed fruit of your womb, Jesus. O clement, O loving, O sweet Virgin Mary.

Prayer to St. Michael

Holy Michael, the Archangel, defend us in battle. Be our safeguard against the wickedness and snares of the devil. May God rebuke him, we humbly pray; and do you, O Prince of the heavenly host, by the power of God cast into hell Satan and all the evil spirits who wander through the world seeking the ruin of souls. Amen.

Morning Offering

O Jesus, through the immaculate heart of Mary, I offer you my prayers, works, joys and sufferings of this day in union with the holy sacrifice of the Mass throughout the world. I offer them for all the intentions of your sacred heart: the salvation of souls, reparation for sin, the reunion of all Christians. I offer them for the intentions of our bishops and of all the apostles of prayer, and in particular for those recommended by our Holy Father this month.

Prayer before Meals

Bless us, O Lord, and these your gifts, which we are about to receive from your bounty, through Christ our Lord. Amen.

Prayer after Meals

We give you thanks for all your benefits, O loving God, you who live and reign forever. Amen.

Act of Spiritual Communion

(Prayed when it isn't possible to receive Communion.)
My Jesus, I believe that you are in the Blessed Sacrament. I love you above all things, and I long for you in my soul. Since I cannot now receive you sacramentally, come at least spiritually into my heart. As though you have already come, I embrace you and unite myself entirely to you; never permit me to be separated from you.

The Divine Praises

Blessed be God.

Blessed be his holy Name.

Blessed be Jesus Christ, true God and true man.

Blessed be the Name of Jesus.

Blessed be his most Sacred Heart.

Blessed be his most Precious Blood.

Blessed be Jesus in the most holy Sacrament of the altar.

Blessed be the Holy Spirit, the Paraclete.

Blessed be the great Mother of God, Mary most holy.

Blessed be her holy and immaculate conception.

Blessed be her glorious assumption.

Blessed be the name of Mary, Virgin and Mother.

Blessed be St. Joseph, her most chaste spouse.

Blessed be God in his angels and in his saints.

Praying the Rosary

The Fatima Prayer may be said at the end of each decade after the Glory: "O my Jesus, forgive us our sins, save us from the fires of hell. Lead all souls to heaven, especially those most in need of thy mercy."

The Joyful Mysteries

The Annunciation—The angel Gabriel announced that God had chosen Mary to be the Mother of Jesus the savior.

The Visitation—Mary visited her older relative Elizabeth who was pregnant with John the Baptist.

The Birth of Jesus—Mary gave birth to Jesus.

The Presentation in the Temple—Mary and Joseph took baby Jesus to the Temple to present him to God.

Finding of the Child Jesus in the Temple—After Passover, Jesus remained in Jerusalem. Three days later his parents found him in the Temple listening to teachers and asking them questions.

The Luminous Mysteries or Mysteries of Light

The Baptism in the Jordan River—Jesus had John the Baptist baptize him. A voice came from heaven saying, "This is my beloved Son."

The Wedding at Cana—At Mary's request Jesus changed water into wine when it ran out.

The Proclamation of the Kingdom of God—Jesus proclaimed the Good News of God's love and salvation.

The Transfiguration—On a mountain with Peter, James, and John, Jesus appeared radiant and spoke with Moses and Elijah.

The Institution of the Eucharist—On the night before he died, Jesus shared a meal with his disciples and gave us the Eucharist.

The Sorrowful Mysteries

The Agony in the Garden—After the Last Supper, Jesus prayed in a garden, "Father, if it is possible, let this cup pass from me; yet, not as I will, but as you will."

The Scourging at the Pillar—To satisfy the crowd, Pontius Pilate had Jesus whipped.

The Crowning with Thorns—Soldiers placed a crown of thorns on Jesus's head, put a reed in his hand, and mocked him as a king.

The Carrying of the Cross—Jesus carried his cross to Calvary. He was helped by Simon of Cyrene when he grew weak.

The Crucifixion—Jesus was nailed to a cross between two criminals and died to save us.

The Glorious Mysteries

The Resurrection—Jesus rose from the dead on the third day, just as he had promised.

The Ascension of Our Lord—Jesus sent his disciples forth to preach the Good News to the whole world, and was then taken up into heaven.

The Descent of the Holy Spirit—The Holy Spirit was poured forth on the disciples as they prayed in the Upper Room on Pentecost.

The Assumption of Our Lady—Mary at the end of her earthly life was taken up body and soul into heavenly glory.

The Coronation of the Blessed Virgin Mary—The holy Mother of God reigns in heaven, where she prays for and cares for us.

Stations of the Cross

First Station—Jesus Condemned to Death

Second Station—Jesus Carries His Cross

Third Station—Jesus Falls the First Time

Fourth Station—Jesus Meets His Mother

Fifth Station—Simon of Cyrene Helps Jesus Carry His Cross

Sixth Station—Veronica Wipes the Face of Jesus

Seventh Station—Jesus Falls the Second Time

Eighth Station—Jesus Consoles the Women of Jerusalem

Ninth Station—Jesus Falls the Third Time

Tenth Station—Jesus Stripped of His Garments

Eleventh Station—Jesus Nailed to the Cross

Twelfth Station—Jesus Dies on the Cross

Thirteenth Station—Jesus Taken Down from the Cross

Fourteenth Station—Jesus Laid in the Tomb

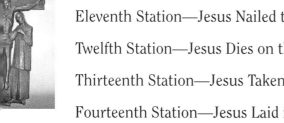

Index

Abba, 222

abortion, 193

Abraham, 16, 19, 20, 78, 89, 170, 185, 207

absolution, 137, 139, 141

Act
of Contrition, 139, 141, 233
of Faith, 8, 232
of Hope, 232
of Love, 232

actual grace, 160

actual sin, 38, 121

Adam, 15, 33, 34, 37–40, 43, 83, 107,
153–154, 159

Adam and Eve, 15, 37–40, 43, 107,
153–154, 159

adultery, 165, 197, 199, 202, 227

Advent, 115

agnosticism, 12

alb, 132

alleluia, 81–82

altar, 19, 117, 132–133, 151, 174, 195

amen, 134, 231

Andrew (apostle) 17, 18, 97, 134

Andrew Dung-Lac, Saint, 97

angel, 19, 34, 36, 45, 46, 50, 52, 53, 79,
106, 108, 113, 131, 174, 222

Angelus, 233

annulment, 155

Annunciation, 50, 101, 237

anointing, 124–127, 129

Anointing of the Sick, sacrament of, 113, 136,
142–147

apostle, 7, 17, 18, 22, 24, 47, 57, 58, 60, 69,
72, 73, 74, 79–84, 87, 91, 101, 109, 113,
119, 125, 126, 131, 134, 137, 142, 148,
150, 151, 152, 156, 167, 218, 221, 225,

Apostles' Creed, 7, 78, 103, 232

Ascension, 72, 81, 112, 182, 183, 238

Assumption, 101, 105, 182, 183, 238

atheism, 12, 172

Aquinas. See Thomas Aquinas, Saint

Augustine, Saint, 6, 28, 81, 82, 88

Baptism, sacrament of, 30, 86, 87, 89, 94,
113, 118–125, 127, 128, 129, 136, 149,
151, 159, 179, 180, 222, 237

baptismal font, 117, 119

beatific vision, 108

beatitudes, 166–167, 169, 228

belief, 4, 7, 8, 12, 68, 78, 159, 171, 172, 174

Bernardine of Siena, Saint, 177

Benedict, Saint, 91

Bernadette Soubirous, Saint, 102

Bible, 17, 21–26, 32, 33, 36, 39, 46, 49, 59,
85, 98, 128, 179, 201, 216

bishop, 6, 7, 17, 18, 29, 90–93, 97, 119,
125, 126, 127, 129, 133, 137, 144,
148–150, 152, 177, 182, 211, 235

blasphemy, 178, 180

blessing, 23, 35, 40, 114, 154, 164, 204,
217, 220

Blessed Sacrament, 132, 235. *See also* Eucharist

Blood of Christ, 22, 95, 134

body, 5, 9, 34, 36, 49, 73, 74, 78, 79, 81, 90, 93, 98, 100, 106, 107, 108, 112, 131, 132

Body of Christ, 22, 89, 90, 94, 95, 130, 131, 132, 134, 183, 198

bread, 69, 73, 80, 99, 113, 130–135, 155, 219, 223,

Calvary, 73–74, 80, 185, 238

cardinal moral virtue, 162, 229

Catechism of the Catholic Church, 2, 3

catechumen, 119–120, 125

Catherine of Siena, Saint, 85

catholic, 91, 94

Catholic Church, the. *See* Church, the

chalice, 132, 134

charity, 62, 86, 121, 162, 171, 194, 204, 229, 230

Charles Lwanga, Saint, 189

chastity, 86, 92, 173, 200, 230

children, 15, 38, 58, 86, 87, 104, 118, 119, 123, 133, 148, 153, 154, 156, 157, 166, 187, 188, 198, 199, 222, 228

Chi–Rho, 45

chrism, 120, 125–127, 144,

Christian, 2, 3, 6, 17, 22, 44, 46, 75, 81, 82, 90, 97, 98, 107, 115, 120, 121, 125, 126, 129, 156, 157, 158, 170, 173, 179, 180, 182, 186, 189, 193, 211, 221

Christmas, 35, 53, 115

Church, the, 4, 6, 7, 17, 18, 20, 22–23, 25, 26, 27, 29, 31, 40, 46, 50, 57, 81, 84, 85, 87, 88, 89–99, 100, 101, 104, 106, 112, 113, 114, 117, 118, 119, 120, 123, 124, 125, 126, 130, 132, 136, 137, 138, 139, 141,

143, 145, 148, 150, 152, 153, 154, 155, 156, 162, 178, 182, 193, 206,

Clare, Saint, 183

clergy, 148, 151

common good, 164, 193

communion, 85, 89, 95, 99, 114, 197

Communion. *See* Holy Communion

Communion of Saints, 95–99, 232

community, 3, 13, 44, 62, 68, 81, 92, 94, 109, 143, 144, 145, 148, 149, 171, 183, 194, 204, 209, 217

compassion, 13, 67, 70, 146, 193,

confession 138, 140, 160. *See also* Penance, sacrament of

Confirmation, sacrament of, 86, 113, 118, 124–129, 149

conscience ,136, 138, 158–161, 163, 188, 191

consecration, 149–150, 152

contrition, 138, 219

conversion, 81, 137

corporal work of mercy, 194, 206, 208, 229

counsel, 92, 127, 173, 230

covenant, 15, 16, 20, 22, 131, 154, 165

Covenant, New, 73, 76

covet, 165, 197, 203, 227

creation, 5, 8, 15, 22, 29, 32–33, 35, 36, 37, 38, 86, 128, 182, 184

creed, 2, 7

cross, 5, 57, 58, 71–76, 101, 103, 131, 137, 149, 171, 190, 238, 239

Cross, Sign of. *See* Sign of the Cross

Cross, Stations of. *See* Stations of the Cross

crucifix, 103

Crucifixion, 185, 238

Damien of Molokai, Saint, 149

deacon, 80, 92, 93, 119, 148–149, 150–152, 154

death, 3, 18, 23, 27, 39, 40, 51, 56, 57, 58, 67, 70, 71–78, 106–107, 109, 111, 112, 119, 127, 130, 131, 135, 137, 143, 144, 145, 154, 157, 159, 193, 239

Decalogue, 165

devotion, 103, 177, 199

dignity, 33, 34, 153, 196, 201, 206

diocese, 125, 150, 182

disciple, 3, 57, 66, 69, 80, 86, 102

Divine Office 51, 115, 221

divine Persons, 28, 83, 232

Divine Praises, 178, 236

Divine Providence, 35

divorce, 155

doctrine, 18

Dominic Savio, Saint, 162

doxology, 223

earth, 4, 10, 12, 17, 18, 29, 32, 33, 34, 35, 39, 43, 44, 45, 46, 59, 70, 77, 89, 90, 95, 96, 99, 100, 104, 105, 107, 109, 116, 118, 130, 154, 166, 174, 188, 190, 191, 203, 208

Easter (Sunday), 73, 77, 79, 80, 81, 84, 114, 115, 120, 183

Easter Vigil, 119

eighth commandment, 165, 209, 211, 212, 214, 227

Elizabeth Ann Seton, Saint, 62

Elizabeth of Hungary, Saint, 155

envy, 159, 206, 208

eternity, 13, 98, 107, 110

Eucharist, 22, 39, 89, 90, 95, 99, 112, 113, 118, 130–135, 145, 149, 151, 152, 154, 181, 183, 184, 186, 200, 215, 223, 237
    sacrament of, 130–135
euthanasia, 193
evangelical counsels, 92, 173
Eve, 15, 33, 37–40, 43, 102, 107, 153–154, 159
evil, 12, 38–40, 68, 70, 96, 120, 158, 160, 164, 178, 193, 204, 221, 223, 226
examination of conscience, 138

faith, 4–8, 12, 17, 18, 19, 22, 29, 49, 57, 58, 61, 67, 69, 70, 77, 80, 85, 89, 91, 94, 95, 97, 99, 102, 107, 114, 115, 119, 120, 121, 123, 125, 126, 129, 140, 143, 145, 146, 150, 162, 171, 172, 179, 183, 188, 211, 214, 216, 217, 218, 229,
family, 15, 23, 29, 39, 43, 96, 156, 164, 171, 186, 189, 205, 206, 222
fasting, 55, 56, 134, 140
fear, 69, 79, 125, 144
fear of the Lord, 127, 230. *See also* reverence
feast day, 7, 13, 18, 24, 29, 35, 44, 51, 57, 62, 68, 72, 80, 85, 91, 97, 102, 108, 115, 120, 126, 133, 140, 149, 155, 162, 173, 177, 183, 189, 200, 204, 211, 217, 224
Felicity, Saint, 120
fifth commandment, 165, 192–196, 227
forgiveness, 73, 131, 133, 226
fortitude, 127, 162, 229, 230
fourth commandment, 165, 187–191, 227
Francis de Sales, Saint, 211, 212
Francis of Assisi, Saint, 35, 183
Francis Xavier, Saint, 126

free will, 34, 37, 40, 71
fruits of the Holy Spirit, 86, 230

Gabriel, Archangel, 50, 237
Genesis, 32, 35, 37, 38, 40, 42, 182
gift, 4, 19, 24, 35, 40, 41, 52, 63, 65, 72, 86, 90, 92, 93, 100, 114, 125, 133, 145, 154, 155, 156, 162, 171, 190, 192, 194, 195, 198, 199, 201, 202, 203, 205, 215, 221, 223
gifts of the Holy Spirit, 121, 124, 126–127, 129, 230
Glory (Be), 31, 103, 231, 237
gluttony, 159
God, nature of, 9–14, 27–29, 46, 48, 49–50, 54, 83, 170, 176–177
godparent, 121, 127
goodness (God's),15, 32, 36
goodness (fruit of Holy Spirit), 86, 230
Good News, 23, 52, 56, 57, 66, 79, 81, 133, 237, 238
Gospel, 17, 22–24, 26, 53, 56, 57, 66, 71, 72, 74, 79, 82, 91, 103, 126, 133, 150, 151, 167, 183, 204, 223
gossip, 212
grace, 37, 38–39, 41, 42, 53, 62, 77, 92, 95, 97, 98, 99, 100, 105, 106, 107, 108, 112, 113, 114, 117, 118, 121, 124, 125, 126, 129, 133, 137, 138, 139, 144, 145, 147, 150, 153, 155, 157, 162, 185, 220, 224
greed, 159, 208
Gregory the Great, Saint, (pope), 115
guilt (feeling of), 136

Hail Mary, 215, 231
happiness, 5, 8, 109, 111, 164, 166, 168, 169
hate, 39
healing, 66, 70, 146, 185
heart, 4, 5, 12, 23, 27, 30, 35, 77, 86, 115, 134, 136, 140, 142, 144, 164, 166, 168, 171, 183, 193, 197, 200, 201, 215, 216, 220
heaven, 4, 5, 6, 12, 18, 21, 29, 30, 32, 33, 35, 40, 42, 43, 44, 47, 77, 79, 81, 82, 95, 96, 98, 99, 100, 101, 106, 107, 108–111, 113, 114, 121, 122, 131, 132, 154, 162, 166, 179, 222, 237, 238
hell, 34, 106, 107, 108–111, 178
heresy, 50
Herod, 39, 52, 54
hierarchy, 92
holiness, 12, 38, 91, 92, 93, 98, 113, 121, 127, 130, 135, 137, 143, 158, 159, 162, 163, 168
Holy Communion, 95, 99, 132, 133, 135, 145, 160, 147, 172, 200, 228, 235
holy day of obligation, 183, 228
Holy Family, 52, 54, 156
Holy Orders, sacrament of, 92, 113, 148–152, 153
Holy Spirit, 17, 23, 27–31, 45, 46, 49, 50, 54, 60, 62, 72, 79, 80, 83–88, 90, 92, 97, 114, 117, 120, 123, 124, 125, 126–129, 135, 137, 145, 150, 159, 162, 198, 238
Holy Thursday, 73, 125
holy water, 28, 114
homily, 133
honor, 23, 46, 53, 81, 132, 172, 190, 198
hope, 16, 40, 86, 98, 107, 121, 144, 162, 171, 172, 229

human nature, 50

human person, 43, 49

humility, 102, 127, 218

idolatry, 172

Ignatius of Loyola, Saint, 43, 44, 126

Immaculate Conception, 40, 100–102, 105, 183

Incarnation, 17, 49, 54, 114

intention, 160, 163, 203

intercession, 97, 217, 220

Isaac Jogues, Saint, 173

Israel, 43, 52, 104, 122, 142, 165

    Israelite, 11, 13, 14, 16, 20, 22, 39, 72, 75, 76, 122, 165, 172

Jacob (patriarch), 16

James (apostle), 17, 57, 72, 146, 237

    James, Letter of, 24, 142, 213

Jesus Christ, 4, 5, 6, 7, 17, 18, 20, 22, 23, 25, 27, 30, 43–82, 90, 94, 112, 132, 135, 149, 177

Jews, 16, 24, 45, 46, 52, 58, 64, 71, 72, 74, 170

John, Gospel of, 23, 24, 30

John (evangelist), 13, 17, 47, 57, 72, 74, 79, 98, 101, 146, 179

John of God, Saint, 144

John Mary Vianney, Saint, 140

John the Baptist, 30, 39, 51, 66, 237

Joseph, Saint, 50, 51–54, 156, 190, 237

joy, 41, 82, 86, 108, 125, 150, 181, 184, 198, 217, 222, 223, 230

Judas (apostle), 17, 72–73

judgment, 12, 106, 127

justice, 12, 33, 35, 36, 109, 162, 188, 190, 193, 205, 222, 229

killing, 5, 193, 196

kindness, 10, 86, 193, 230

kingdom (of God), 34–35, 45, 50, 55, 56, 58, 60, 61, 62–63, 65, 66–70, 74, 81, 87, 89, 90, 92, 106, 109, 118, 146, 166, 169, 193, 204, 221–223, 226, 228, 237

knowledge, 5, 11, 13, 38, 53, 83, 127, 230

laity, 92

Lamb of God, 72, 76, 98, 179

last judgment, 109

Last Supper, 73, 76, 83, 131, 135, 167, 238

law (of God), 7, 16, 20, 39, 52, 58, 90, 164–169, 172, 188, 191, 193

laying on of hands, 124–126, 129, 147, 149, 152

leaders (of the Church), 7, 18, 57, 58, 59, 91, 189

lectio divina, 219, 220

Lent, 56, 73, 115, 171

lie, 209–210

litany, 99, 225

liturgical season, 115

liturgical year, 114, 115, 117

liturgy, 112–117, 131,
    Liturgy of the Eucharist, 133
    Liturgy of the Hours, 51, 224
    Liturgy of the Word, 21, 26, 133, 145

Lord, 7, 12, 36, 46, 48, 75, 85, 176, 190, 192

Lord's Day, the, 114, 181–186

Lord's Prayer, the, 215, 221

love, 5, 6, 11, 13, 22, 29, 32, 33, 35, 36, 37, 39, 43, 49, 50, 59, 71, 86, 87, 91, 95, 99, 103, 109, 114, 140, 143, 145, 149, 153–154, 156–157, 159, 162, 164, 167, 170–175, 177, 193, 194–195, 197–202, 206, 219, 222, 230

Luke, Gospel of, 23, 56

Luke (evangelist), 24

lust, 159

Magi, 52

magisterium, 18

Magnificat, 51, 54

Maria Goretti, Saint, 200

Mark, Gospel of, 23, 116

marks
    of the church, 91
    of confirmation, 127

marriage, 151, 153–157, 173, 178, 197–201

Martin de Porres, Saint, 68

martyr, 7, 97, 98, 173, 189, 211
    martyrdom, 39, 151

Mary (mother of Jesus), 39, 40, 42, 44, 49–54, 57, 71, 72, 74, 84, 87, 100–105, 114, 124, 156, 172, 177, 182, 183, 190, 200, 222, 231, 233, 234, 236, 237, 238
    Queen, 101–103, 234

Mary Magdalene, Saint, 57, 79

Mass, 26, 96, 112, 115, 125, 130–135, 144, 171, 182–186, 216, 217, 228. *See also* Eucharist; liturgy

Matrimony, sacrament of, 113, 153–157

Matthew, Gospel of, 23, 66, 158, 167, 204, 223

Matthew (evangelist), 17, 58

media, 212

meditation, 216, 220

meek, 166, 228

Memorare, 234

    mercy, 13, 15, 16, 39, 40, 41, 42, 43, 47, 159, 166, 181

    in the beatitudes, 228, 229

    prayers for, 233, 234, 237

    See also work of mercy

Messiah, 45, 52, 56, 66, 70

miracle, 56, 60, 66–70, 80, 97, 134, 183

missionary, 91, 92, 126, 149, 173, 194

modesty, 86, 230

monk, 91, 115

moral act, 158

morality, 160. *See also* cardinal moral virtue; virtue

Morning Offering, 235

mortal sin, 108, 161

Moses, 11, 16, 57, 75, 78, 122, 165, 167, 172, 176, 178, 237

Mother of God. *See* Mary (mother of Jesus)

murder, 172. *See also* killing

mystery, 10, 15, 27–28, 49, 103, 179

    Joyful Mysteries, 237

    Glorious Mysteries, 238

    Luminous or Mysteries of Light, 237

    Sorrowful Mysteries, 238

    See also Paschal Mystery

Mystical Body of Christ, 90, 94, 100

name

    God's name, 11, 12, 14, 165, 176–180, 227

    Holy Spirit's name, 83, 86

    in Baptism, 97, 98, 119–120

    Jesus's name, 44–45, 47, 49, 50, 57, 69

    Mary's name, 100–101

natural law, 164–165

nature, 12, 36, 69, 70

neighbor, 64, 162, 165, 168, 197, 203, 209, 227

New Testament, 22, 26, 204

Nicene Creed, 7

ninth commandment, 165, 197–202, 227

Noah, 15–16, 39

non–Christians

    Jews, 9, 12, 16, 25, 26, 43, 46, 52, 58, 59, 64, 71, 72, 116, 168, 170, 176

    Muslims, 170, 176

novena, 216

nun, 91, 224. *See also* sister

oaths, 178, 210

obedience, 19, 92, 173, 187–191

octave, 216

    Church Unity Octave, 90

oil, 45, 85, 86, 113, 124, 125, 129, 142, 143, 145, 147

    chrism, 120, 125

    oil of catechumens, 120, 125

    oil of the sick, 125, 144

Old Testament, 22, 26, 83, 89, 149, 199

omnipotent, 10

omnipresent, 10

omniscient, 10

ordination, 149–150, 152

original justice, 37

original sin,, 37–39, 40, 42, 43, 89

Our Father, 2, 41, 103, 177, 221–226, 231

pain, 38, 109, 199

parable, 22–23, 25, 56, 60–65, 137, 146, 204, 207, 219

Paraclete, 85, 236

paradise, 33, 37–42

parent, 53, 121, 156, 164, 188, 190

first parents (Adam and Eve), 15, 37, 42, 154

parish, 35, 89, 94, 119, 126, 150, 151, 183

particular judgment, 107, 111

Pasch, the, 72

paschal candle, 117, 120

paschal mystery, 72, 77, 112, 114, 119, 183

Passion, the, 112, 143, 233

Passover, 53, 72, 73, 131, 237

pastor, 150

patience, 86, 230

Patrick, Saint, 28, 29

patron saint, 97–98, 99, 123, 173, 180

Paul, Saint, 24, 39, 44, 48, 80–81, 92, 93, 106, 154

peace, 35, 36, 86, 104, 109, 115, 126, 139, 144, 190, 193, 214, 222, 230

    peacemaker, 166, 228

    Prince of Peace, 195

penance, 104, 140, 143

Penance, sacrament of, 113, 126, 136–141, 144, 172, 200, 228, 233

Pentecost, 27, 29, 84, 86, 88, 89, 101, 124, 125, 238

People of God, 35, 89–90, 148

perjury, 178, 180, 210

Perpetua, Saint, 120

Peter, Saint, 17, 18, 24, 45, 46, 47, 57, 72, 74, 79, 80, 84, 146, 151, 190, 237

petition, 25, 217, 219, 220, 222, 223

pharaoh, 11, 16, 122

Pharisees, 58

piety, 127, 230

Pilate, Pontius, 73, 232, 238

Pio of Pietrelcina, Saint, 108

Pius X, Saint, 133

poor, 56, 66, 148, 160, 166, 206, 228

pope, 7, 18, 90, 92, 93, 97, 150, 167

poverty, 92, 173

praise, 25, 54, 98, 114, 131, 133, 171, 182, 183, 217, 219, 223

prayer, 6, 8, 25, 39, 44, 62, 70, 143, 171, 177, 184, 215–220

preaching, 30, 61

precepts, 168, 228

pride, 159

priest, 45, 90, 92, 112, 115, 120, 127, 130, 132, 136, 137, 138, 139, 143, 148–150, 200

profanity, 178, 180

promise, 12, 15, 20, 51, 83, 91, 119, 120, 126, 162, 173, 188, 197, 211

property, 203, 208

prophet, 16, 45, 56, 57, 90, 120, 174

prudence, 162, 229

psalm, 25, 26, 100, 116 133, 216, 220

punishment, 121, 138, 139, 193

purgatory, 95, 96, 99, 107, 108, 111

purity, 77

rash judgment, 211, 214

RCIA. See Right of Christian Initiation of Adults

readings. See Liturgy of the Word

reconciliation, 137, 139, 195

Reconciliation, sacrament of. See Penance, sacrament of

Redeemer, 40, 43, 55, 73, 182

redemption, 13, 114, 120, 131, 184

religion, 171

repentance, 137, 145

respect, 12, 127, 149, 176–180, 187–196, 198–199, 201–202, 203, 208, 212

responsibility, 125, 129, 188, 206, 212

resurrection (of Christ), 23, 40, 56, 67, 72, 77–82, 83, 112, 114, 130–131, 135, 137, 150, 151, 182, 238

revelation, 15, 17, 20, 170

Revelation, Book of, 22, 72, 98, 104, 110

reverence, 176–177, 230. See also fear of the Lord

right, 58, 121, 192–193, 196, 203, 208, 209

rite, 115, 119
   of Anointing of the Sick, 147
   of Baptism, 120
   of Confirmation, 126
   the Mass, 133
   penitential, 139

Rite of Christian Initiation of Adults, 119, 123

Roman (rite), 115

Rosary (prayer), 103, 105, 237

Rose Philippine, Saint, 217

Sabbath, 58, 182, 185

sacrament, 39, 62, 85, 99, 112, 113–114, 236
   of healing, 136
   of initiation, 118–119, 124, 130
   of service, 148, 153
   See also Anointing of the Sick, Baptism, Confirmation, Eucharist, Holy Orders, Matrimony, Penance

sacramental, 114

sacramental grace, 114

Sacred Heart (of Jesus), 50, 235, 236

sacrifice, 19, 58, 130, 131, 132, 149, 171, 175, 189

sacrilege, 172, 175

Sadducees, 58

saint, 6, 62, 96–97, 179, 216, 222, 236. See also Communion of Saints; patron saint

salvation, 16, 72, 98, 237

sanctifying grace, 29, 31, 121

scandal, 194

Scripture, 13, 17, 21, 23, 85, 160, 179

second commandment, 165, 176–178, 180, 227

sermon, 18

Sermon on the Mount, 167–168

service, 112, 151

seven gifts of the Holy Spirit, 126, 128

seven sacraments, 113, 117. See also sacrament

seventh commandment, 165, 201, 205, 227

sexuality, 198–202

Sign of the Cross, 28, 76, 103, 120, 145, 231

sinner, 41, 56, 136, 140, 229

sin, 15, 39, 41, 42, 49, 71, 72, 73, 76, 86, 161, 162, 163, 172, 175, 178, 180, 192–193, 194, 196, 199, 202, 211, 223, 232–237
   See also mortal sin; venial sin; social sin; original sin

sister (religious), 102, 183, 194, 211, 217. See also nun

sixth commandment, 165, 197–202, 227

slavery, 20, 72–73, 122, 161

sloth, 159

social sin, 161

society, 153, 156, 189, 190, 199, 209

Son of God, 17, 43, 46, 50, 55, 59, 77

soul, 34, 36, 96, 100, 106, 107, 113, 126, 136, 168

spirit, 9, 14, 30, 34, 36, 49, 57, 68, 74, 80, 128, 206
   See also Holy Spirit

spiritual work of mercy, 206, 229

sponsor (confirmation), 127

Stations of the Cross, 75, 239

stealing, 5, 160, 164, 165, 203–226, 227

Stephen, Saint, 80

stole (vestment), 132, 150–151

suffering, 34, 37, 39, 66, 70, 72–74, 96, 108, 120, 143, 144, 147, 149, 193

suicide, 193

Sunday, 182–186

supernatural, 29

superstition, 173

swear, 178

symbol, 23, 28, 45, 50, 71, 75, 79, 85, 86, 104, 114, 118, 120, 125, 150, 177, 210

tabernacle, 87, 132

talent, 63

teacher, 6, 18, 88

temperance, 162, 229

temptation, 39, 41, 55, 68, 138, 139, 144, 147, 150, 160, 183, 200, 223

Ten Commandments, 16, 138, 165–167, 169, 227

tenth commandment, 165, 203–208, 227

Teresa of Avila, Saint, 224

Teresa of Calcutta, Blessed, 194

thanksgiving, 116, 131, 217, 220

theological virtue. *See* virtue; faith; hope; love

third commandment, 165, 181–186, 227

Thomas Aquinas, Saint, 13

Thomas More, Saint, 167, 178

tradition, 17, 20, 50, 51, 85

Transfiguration, 57, 72, 237

transubstantiation, 131

Triduum, 73, 216

Trinity, 27–31, 43, 48, 83, 88, 121, 153

trust, 34, 144, 173, 197, 203, 209

truth, 12, 85, 165, 178, 190, 209–214, 216

Twelve, the (apostles), 17, 57, 60

understanding, 17, 127, 195, 230

unity, 89–91, 96, 130, 150, 153, 183

universal Church, 51, 90, 91

venerable, 96

venial sin, 138, 161

vestments, 132

Vicar of Christ, 18, 90, 150

vice, 159, 163

Vincent de Paul, Saint, 97, 204

virtue, 9, 62, 65, 97, 121, 156, 162–163, 171, 179, 180, 188, 200, 229

    cardinal moral virtue, 162, 229

    theological virtue, 162, 229

vocation, 152, 159, 184, 200

vow, 68, 92, 120, 150, 154, 157, 170, 173, 175, 199, 201

war, 193

water, 28, 30, 68, 69, 75, 85–87, 102, 113, 118–120, 122, 123, 128, 130, 134, 156, 237

will (of God), 37, 38, 41, 55, 73, 190, 221–222, 225–226, 238

wine, 64, 69, 73, 99, 102, 130–135, 156

wisdom, 127, 230

wise men, 52

witness, 7, 81, 125, 144, 183, 211

Word of God, 17–18, 23, 26, 120, 223

work of God (Jesus or Holy Spirit), 29, 35, 46, 62, 83, 85, 112–113, 143, 159

works of mercy, 194, 206, 208. *See also* corporal works of mercy; spiritual works of mercy

worship ,17, 91, 112–113, 116–117, 131, 135, 150, 171, 172, 175, 180, 182, 184

wrath, 64, 159

Acknowledgments

Public Domain images courtesy of WikiMedia Commons, accessed August through November 2012

Ludolf Backhuysen — Christ in the Storm on the Sea of Galilee, 1695. http://commons.wikimedia.org/wiki/File%3ABackhuysen,_Ludolf_-_Christ_in_the_Storm_on_the_Sea_of_Galilee_-_1695.jpg. p. 66.

Alexander Bida — Jesus Anointing, 1874. http://commons.wikimedia.org/wiki/File:Jesus_Anointing.jpg. p. 140

William Blake —The Ancient of Days, 1794. http://commons.wikimedia.org/wiki/File:Letters_of_William_Blake,_page_34_%28The_Ancient_of_Days%29.jpeg. p. half-title

Carl Heinrich Bloch —The Annunciation, 1865. http://commons.wikimedia.org/wiki/File:Carl_Heinrich_Bloch_-_The_Annunciation.jpg. p. 50

Carl Heinrich Bloch —The Transfiguration, 1872. http://commons.wikimedia.org/wiki/File:Transfiguration_bloch.jpg. p. 57

Carl Heinrich Bloch — The Resurrection, 1873. http://commons.wikimedia.org/wiki/File:Carl_Heinrich_Bloch_-_The_Resserection.jpg. p. 78

Carl Heinrich Bloch — The Sermon on the Mount, 1877. http://en.wikipedia.org/wiki/File:Bloch-SermonOnTheMount.jpg. p. 61

Carl Heinrich Bloch — The Last Supper, 1876. http://commons.wikimedia.org/wiki/File:The-Last-Supper-large.jpg. p. 73

Jan de Bray — The Holy Family, second half of the 17th century, http://commons.wikimedia.org/wiki/File:Jan_de_Bray_-_The_Holy_Family_-_WGA3126.jpg. p. 43

Hendrick ter Brugghen —The Supper at Emmaus, c. 1621. http://commons.wikimedia.org/wiki/File:The_supper_at_Emmaus.jpg. p. 80

Karoly Ferenczy — Sermon on the Mount, 1896. http://commons.wikimedia.org/wiki/File:Ferenczy,_K%C3%A1roly_-_Sermon_on_the_Mountain_%281896%29.jpg. p. 166

Benventuo Tisi da Garofalo — Ascension of Christ, between 1510-1520. http://commons.wikimedia.org/wiki/File:Benvenuto_Tisi_da_Garofalo_-_Ascension_of_Christ_-_WGA08474.jpg. p. 81

Manuel Gómez-Moreno González — San Juan de Dios salvando del incendio a los enfermos del Hospital Real de Granada, 1880. http://commons.wikimedia.org/wiki/File:Manuel_G%C3%B3mez-Moreno_Gonz%C3%A1lez._San_Juan_de_Dios_salvando_a_los_enfermos_de_incendio_del_Hospital_Real_%281880%29.jpg. p. 144

Benozzo Gozzoli — Madonna and Child between St. Francis and St. Bernardine of Siena, 1450 http://commons.wikimedia.org/wiki/File:Benozzo_Gozzoli_-_Madonna_and_Child_between_St_Francis_and_St_Bernardine_of_Siena_-_WGA10215.jpg. p. 177

Paul Hoecker — Mariae Verkundigung (Annunciation to Mary), 1890. http://commons.wikimedia.org/wiki/File:Glaspalast_M%C3%BCnchen_1890_103.jpg. p. 49

William Hole — Zacchaeus in Tree, 1908. http://commons.wikimedia.org/wiki/File:Hole_zacchaeus_in_tree.gif. p. 207

Bernardino Luini, The Magdalen, between 1520-1525, http://commons.wikimedia.org/wiki/File:Bernardino_Luini_-_The_Magdalen_-_WGA13766.jpg. p. 57

Bernardino Luini — Madonna mit Kind und Martha, Johannes und Einer Nonne, (Madonna with Child and Young St John and another nun) , c. 1518, http://commons.wikimedia.org/wiki/File:Bernardino_Luini_003.jpg. p. 100

Sebastian del Piombo —Visitation, 1518-1519, http://commons.wikimedia.org/wiki/File:Piombo,_Sebastiano_del_-_The_Visitation_-_1518-19.jpg . p. 51

Louis Rhead — Robin Shoots with Sir Guy, 1912. http://commons.wikimedia.org/wiki/File:Robin_shoots_with_sir_Guy_by_Louis_Rhead_1912.png. p. 203

James Tissot — He Heals the Lame, 1886-1894. http://commons.wikimedia.org/wiki/File:Brooklyn_Museum_-_He_Heals_the_Lame_%28Il_gu%C3%A9rit_les_boiteux%29_-_James_Tissot.jpg. p. 46

James Tissot — Jesus Among the Doctors, 1886-1894. http://commons.wikimedia.org/wiki/File:Brooklyn_Museum_-_Jesus_Among_the_Doctors_%28J%C3%A9sus_parmi_les_docteurs%29_-_James_Tissot_-_overall.jpg. p. 53

James Tissot — Jesus Tempted in the Wilderness, 1886-1894. http://commons.wikimedia.org/wiki/File:Brooklyn_Museum_-_Jesus_Tempted_in_the_Wilderness_%28J%C3%A9sus_tent%C3%A9_dans_le_d%C3%A9sert%29_-_James_Tissot_-_overall.jpg. p. 55

James Tissot — Jesus Unrolls the Book in the Synagogue, 1886-1894. http://commons.wikimedia.org/wiki/File:Brooklyn_Museum_-_Jesus_Unrolls_the_Book_in_the_Synagogue_%28J%C3%A9sus_dans_la_synagogue_d%C3%A9roule_le_livre%29_-_James_Tissot_-_overall.jpg. p. 56

James Tissot — Jesus and the Little Child, 1886-1894. http://commons.wikimedia.org/wiki/File:Brooklyn_Museum_-_Jesus_and_the_Little_Child_%28J%C3%A9sus_et_le_petit_enfant%29_-_James_Tissot_-_overall.jpg. p. 59

James Tissot — The Possessed Boy at the Foot of Mount Tabor, 1886-1894. http://commons.wikimedia.org/wiki/File:Brooklyn_Museum_-_Le_poss%C3%A9d%C3%A9_au_pied_du_Thabor_%28The_Possessed_Boy_at_the_Foot_of_Mount_Tabor%29_-_James_Tissot.jpg. p. 68

James Tissot — Jesus Stilling the Tempest, 1886-1894. http://commons.wikimedia.org/wiki/File:Brooklyn_Museum_-_Jesus_Stilling_the_Tempest_%28J%C3%A9sus_calmant_la_temp%C3%AAte%29_-_James_Tissot_-_overall.jpg. p. 69

James Tissot —The Title on the Cross, 1886-1894. http://commons.wikimedia.org/wiki/File:Brooklyn_Museum_-_The_Title_on_the_Cross_%28Titre_de_la_Croix%29_-_James_Tissot.jpg. p. 71

James Tissot — The Death of Jesus, 1886-1894. http://commons.wikimedia.org/wiki/File:Brooklyn_Museum_-_The_Death_of_Jesus_%28La_mort_de_J%C3%A9sus%29_-_James_Tissot.jpg. p. 74

James Tissot — Jesus Appears to the Holy Women, 1886-1894. http://commons.wikimedia.org/wiki/File:Brooklyn_Museum_-_Jesus_Appears_to_the_Holy_Women_%28Apparition_de_J%C3%A9sus_aux_saintes_femmes%29_-_James_Tissot.jpg. p. 79

James Tissot — Feed My Lambs, 1886-1894. http://commons.wikimedia.org/wiki/File:Brooklyn_Museum_-_Feed_My_Lambs_%28Pais_mes_brebis%29_-_James_Tissot.jpg. p. 151

Other images courtesy of

William Hole — Jesus breaking bread and giving his disciples the cup, c. 1905. A Voz do Silêncio http://voxsilencio.blogspot.com/2010/03/semana-santa-4-feira-participemos-da.html . p. 131

Daughters of St. Paul—pp. 18, 40, 92, 124, 132, 134, 143, 145, 239; Mary Emmanuel Alves, FSP—pp. 3, 10, 15, 77, 96, 112, 113, 133, 148, 150, 151, 153, 154, 171, 176, 177, 184, 187, 188, 189, 192, 195, 210, 215, 218; ; Tracey Matthia Dugas, FSP—p. 173; Ancilla Christine Hirsch, FSP—p. 148; Mary Joseph Peterson, FSP— pp. e, 3, 4, 21, 22, 28, 32, 86, 89, 98, 101, 103, 107, 109, 119, 121, 125, 137, 139, 181, 205, 240; Virginia Helen Richards, FSP—p. 231; Armanda Santos, FSP—p. 130; Nancy Michael Usselmann, FSP—p. 92;

Kevin Galvin—p. 206

Barbara Kiwak —p. 194

Ed and Chris Kumler—p. 153

G. Quaglini—p. 130

Visual Horizons—p. 5, 45

Courtesy of *Saints, Signs, and Symbols* by W. Ellwood Post—cover, pp. c, 44, 45, 72, 85

A special thanks to Sr. Laura Nolin for her invaluable assistance in image research, scanning, and modeling.
"God bless you!"

Who are the Daughters of St. Paul?

We are Catholic sisters. Our mission is to be like Saint Paul and tell everyone about Jesus! There are so many ways for people to communicate with each other. We want to use all of them so everyone will know how much God loves us. We do this by printing books (you're holding one!), making radio shows, singing, helping people at our bookstores, using the Internet, and in many other ways.

Visit our Web site at www.pauline.org

BOOKS & MEDIA

The Daughters of St. Paul operate book and media centers at the following addresses. Visit, call, or write the one nearest you today, or find us at www.pauline.org.

CALIFORNIA

3908 Sepulveda Blvd, Culver City, CA 90230	310-397-8676
935 Brewster Avenue, Redwood City, CA 94063	650-369-4230
5945 Balboa Avenue, San Diego, CA 92111	858-565-9181

FLORIDA

| 145 S.W. 107th Avenue, Miami, FL 33174 | 305-559-6715 |

HAWAII

| 1143 Bishop Street, Honolulu, HI 96813 | 808-521-2731 |

ILLINOIS

| 172 North Michigan Avenue, Chicago, IL 60601 | 312-346-4228 |

LOUISIANA

| 4403 Veterans Memorial Blvd, Metairie, LA 70006 | 504-887-7631 |

MASSACHUSETTS

| 885 Providence Hwy, Dedham, MA 02026 | 781-326-5385 |

MISSOURI

| 9804 Watson Road, St. Louis, MO 63126 | 314-965-3512 |

NEW YORK

| 64 W. 38th Street, New York, NY 10018 | 212-754-1110 |

SOUTH CAROLINA

| 243 King Street, Charleston, SC 29401 | 843-577-0175 |

TEXAS

Currently no book center; for parish exhibits or outreach evangelization, contact: 210-569-0500 or SanAntonio@paulinemedia.com

VIRGINIA

| 1025 King Street, Alexandria, VA 22314 | 703-549-3806 |

CANADA

| 3022 Dufferin Street, Toronto, ON M6B 3T5 | 416-781-9131 |

THE END